BANKING AND BANKING DEVELOPMENTS SERIES

THE BANK SECRECY ACT: INFORMATION SHARING AND SECURITY EFFORTS

BANKING AND BANKING DEVELOPMENTS SERIES

Financial Institutions in Turmoil
Carl D. Aspelin (Editor)
2010. ISBN: 978-1-60692-044-2

Finance and Banking Developments
Charles V. Karsone (Editor)
2010. ISBN: 978-1-60876-329-0

The Bank Secrecy Act : Information Sharing and Security Efforts
Leif Ekstrom (Editor)
2010. ISBN: 978-1-60741-983-9

BANKING AND BANKING DEVELOPMENTS SERIES

THE BANK SECRECY ACT: INFORMATION SHARING AND SECURITY EFFORTS

LEIF EKSTROM
EDITOR

Nova Science Publishers, Inc.
New York

For permission to use material from this book please contact us:
Telephone 631-231-7269; Fax 631-231-8175
Web Site: http://www.novapublishers.com

LIBRARY OF CONGRESS CATALOGING-IN-PUBLICATION DATA

The Bank Secrecy Act : information sharing and security efforts / editor, Leif Ekstrom.
p. cm.
Includes bibliographical references and index.
ISBN 978-1-60741-983-9 (hardcover : alk. paper)
1. United States. Currency and Foreign Transactions Reporting Act 2. Banks and banking--Records and correspondence--Law and legislation--United States. 3. Banks and banking--Security measures--United States. 4. Confidential communications--Banking--United States. 5. Banking law--United States. I. Ekstrom, Leif.
KF1030.R3B36 2009
346.73'082--dc22

2009036567

Published by Nova Science Publishers, Inc. ✦ New York

CONTENTS

PREFACE

This book explores the Bank Secrecy Act (BSA), which is a legislative framework for combating money laundering. The Financial Crimes Enforcement Network (FinCEN) is responsible for the administration of the BSA regulatory structure, and has delegated examination responsibility to the federal banking regulators. This book describes how BSA compliance and enforcement responsibilities are distributed, how agencies other than FinCEN are implementing those responsibilities and the evaluation of their coordination efforts. This book also discusses security policies and controls for systems at three organizations to evaluate whether security controls effectively protect the confidentiality, integrity and availability of the information and systems that support FinCEN's mission.This book consists of public documents which have been located, gathered, combined, reformatted, and enhanced with a subject index, selectively edited and bound to provide easy access

Chapter 1 - The Financial Crimes Enforcement Network (FinCEN), a bureau within the Department of the Treasury, relies extensively on its own computer systems, as well as those at the Internal Revenue Service (IRS) and the Treasury Communications System (TCS), to administer the Bank Secrecy Act (BSA) and fulfill its mission of safeguarding the U.S. financial system from financial crimes. Effective information security controls over these systems are essential to ensuring that BSA data, which contains sensitive financial information used by law enforcement agencies to prosecute financial crime, is protected from inappropriate or deliberate misuse, improper disclosure, or destruction.

GAO evaluated whether security controls that effectively protect the confidentiality, integrity, and availability of the information and systems that support FinCEN's mission have been implemented. To do this, GAO examined security policies and controls for systems at three organizations.

Chapter 2 - The legislative framework for combating money laundering began with the Bank Secrecy Act (BSA) in 1970 and most recently expanded in 2001with the USA PATRIOT Act. The Financial Crimes Enforcement Network (FinCEN) administers BSA and relies on multiple federal and state agencies to ensure financial institution compliance. GAO was asked to (1) describe how BSA compliance and enforcement responsibilities are distributed, (2) describe how agencies other than FinCEN are implementing those responsibilities and evaluate their coordination efforts, and (3) evaluate how FinCEN is implementing its BSA responsibilities. Among other things, GAO reviewed legislation, past GAO and Treasury reports, and agreements and guidance from all relevant agencies; and interviewed agency, association, and financial institution officials.

In: The Bank Secrecy Act: Information Sharing… ISBN: 978-1-60741-983-9
Editor: Leif Ekstrom

Chapter 1

INFORMATION SECURITY: FURTHER ACTIONS NEEDED TO ADDRESS RISKS TO BANK SECRECY ACT DATA

U. S. Government Accountability Office

WHY GAO DID THIS STUDY

The Financial Crimes Enforcement Network (FinCEN), a bureau within the Department of the Treasury, relies extensively on its own computer systems, as well as those at the Internal Revenue Service (IRS) and the Treasury Communications System (TCS), to administer the Bank Secrecy Act (BSA) and fulfill its mission of safeguarding the U.S. financial system from financial crimes. Effective information security controls over these systems are essential to ensuring that BSA data, which contains sensitive financial information used by law enforcement agencies to prosecute financial crime, is protected from inappropriate or deliberate misuse, improper disclosure, or destruction.

GAO evaluated whether security controls that effectively protect the confidentiality, integrity, and availability of the information and systems that support FinCEN's mission have been implemented. To do this, GAO examined security policies and controls for systems at three organizations.

WHAT GAO RECOMMENDS

GAO recommends that the Secretary of the Treasury direct the FinCEN Director to take several actions to fully implement an effective agencywide information security program. In commenting on a draft of this report, Treasury agreed to develop a detailed corrective action plan for each of the recommendations.

WHAT GAO FOUND

FinCEN, TCS, and IRS have taken important steps in implementing numerous controls to protect the information and systems that support FinCEN's mission; however, significant information security weaknesses remain in protecting the confidentiality, integrity, and availability of these systems and information. The three organizations implemented many information security controls to protect the information and systems that support FinCEN's mission. For example, IRS controlled changes to a key application and FinCEN segregated areas of its network. Nonetheless, the organizations had inconsistently applied or not fully implemented controls to prevent, limit, or detect unauthorized access to this information and these systems. For example, the organizations did not always (1) implement user and password management controls for properly identifying and authenticating users, (2) restrict user access to data to only what was required for performing job functions, (3) adequately encrypt data, (4) protect the external and internal boundaries on its systems, and (5) log user activity on databases. Furthermore, weaknesses in which systems were insecurely configured and patches were not applied to critical systems also existed. As a result, sensitive information used by the federal government, financial institutions, and law enforcement agencies to combat money laundering and terrorist financing is at an increased risk of unauthorized use, modification, or disclosure.

A key reason for many of the weaknesses was that FinCEN and IRS had not fully implemented key information security program activities. For example, FinCEN did not always include detailed implementation guidance in its policies and procedures and adequately test and evaluate information security controls. Furthermore, GAO has previously reported that IRS did not sufficiently verify whether remedial actions were implemented or effective in mitigating vulnerabilities and recommended that it implement a revised remedial action verification process.

ABBREVIATIONS

BSA	Bank Secrecy Act
FinCEN	Financial Crimes Enforcement Network
FISMA	Federal Information Security Management Act
IRS	Internal Revenue Service
NIST	National Institute of Standards and Technology
OMB	Office of Management and Budget
TCS	Treasury Communications System
Treasury	Department of the Treasury
WebCBRS	Web-based Currency and Banking Retrieval System

January 30, 2009

The Honorable Barney Frank
Chairman

The Honorable Spencer Bachus
Ranking Member
Committee on Financial Services
House of Representatives

The Honorable William Lacy Clay
House of Representatives

The Honorable Stephen F. Lynch
House of Representatives

As the administrator of the Bank Secrecy Act (BSA),[1] the Financial Crimes Enforcement Network (FinCEN), a bureau within the Department of the Treasury (Treasury), is tasked with the mission of safeguarding the U.S. financial system from money laundering, terrorist financing, and other abuses. In fulfilling this mission, FinCEN performs analysis in support of law enforcement; issues regulations and enforces compliance with the BSA; facilitates information-sharing of BSA data; and coordinates with foreign counterparts.

FinCEN relies extensively on its own information systems, as well as on systems located at the Treasury components of the Internal Revenue Service (IRS) and the Treasury Communications System (TCS) to manage, store, and disseminate the data that financial institutions are required to report under the

BSA. These data contain sensitive information, including transaction amounts, account numbers, and social security numbers, and are used by law enforcement agencies investigating financial crimes, including terrorist financing and money laundering. The computer systems that support FinCEN's mission must be properly protected through strong information security controls[2] because a security breach could place sensitive financial and personally identifiable information at risk and allow criminals to subvert law enforcement's ability to detect illegal activity.

Our objective was to determine whether information security controls have been implemented that effectively protect the confidentiality, integrity, and availability of the information and systems that support FinCEN's mission. To accomplish this objective, we examined the information security controls at FinCEN and two organizations that operate systems or process and store data on its behalf—specifically, TCS and IRS. We concentrated our evaluation on the applications, databases, and network and mainframe infrastructure that support FinCEN's mission. We performed our review at FinCEN and TCS facilities in the Washington, D.C., metropolitan area and at an IRS computing center.

We conducted this performance audit from March 2008 to January 2009 in accordance with generally accepted government auditing standards. Those standards require that we plan and perform the audit to obtain sufficient, appropriate evidence to provide a reasonable basis for our findings and conclusions based on our audit objective. We believe that the evidence obtained provides a reasonable basis for our findings and conclusions based on our audit objective. For more details on our objective, scope, and methodology, see appendix I.

RESULTS IN BRIEF

Although FinCEN, TCS, and IRS have taken important steps in implementing numerous controls to protect the information and systems that support FinCEN's mission, significant weaknesses existed that impaired their ability to ensure the confidentiality, integrity, and availability of these information and systems. The organizations have implemented many security controls to protect the information and systems. For example, FinCEN employed controls to segregate areas of its network and restrict access to sensitive areas, and IRS controlled changes to a key application in its BSA processing environment. However, weaknesses existed that placed sensitive data at risk of unauthorized disclosure. The organizations did not always consistently apply or fully implement controls to prevent, limit, or detect unauthorized access to devices or systems. For example, the organizations had not consistently or fully (1) implemented user and password management controls for properly identifying and authenticating users, (2) restricted user access to data to permit only the access needed to perform job functions, (3) encrypted data, (4) protected external and internal boundaries, and (5) logged user activity on key systems. Shortcomings also existed in managing system configurations, patching systems, and planning for service continuity. As a result, increased risk exists that unauthorized individuals could read, copy, delete, add, and modify data and disrupt service on systems supporting FinCEN's mission.

A key reason for many of the weaknesses was that FinCEN and IRS had not fully implemented key information security program activities. For example, FinCEN did not always include detailed implementation guidance in its policies and procedures or adequately test and evaluate information security controls. Furthermore, IRS did not sufficiently verify whether actions taken to remedy or mitigate known vulnerabilities were fully implemented or effective.

To help strengthen information security controls over the information and systems supporting FinCEN's mission, we are making five recommendations to the Secretary of the Treasury to direct the Director of FinCEN to fully implement key information security program activities. We also are making 88 recommendations in a separate report with limited distribution. These recommendations consist of actions to be taken to correct the specific information security weaknesses at FinCEN, TCS, and IRS.

In commenting on a draft of this report, Treasury's Deputy Assistant Secretary for Information Systems and Chief Information Officer stated that securely maintaining BSA information contributes to the department's goal of promoting the nation's security through strengthened financial systems. He also stated that Treasury will provide a detailed corrective action plan for each of the recommendations and noted that many of the actions required to address the recommendations are already completed or under way.

BACKGROUND

Information security is a critical consideration for any organization that depends on information systems and computer networks to carry out its mission or business. It is especially important for government agencies, where the public's trust is essential. The dramatic expansion in computer interconnectivity and the rapid increase in the use of the Internet are changing the way our government, the nation, and much of the world communicate and conduct business. Without proper safeguards, they also pose enormous risks that make it easier for individuals and groups with malicious intent to intrude into inadequately protected systems and use such access to obtain sensitive information, commit fraud, disrupt operations, or launch attacks against other computer systems and networks.

Our previous reports, and those by inspectors general, describe serious and widespread information security control deficiencies that continue to place federal assets at risk of inadvertent or deliberate misuse, mission-critical information at risk of unauthorized modification or destruction, sensitive information at risk of inappropriate disclosure, and critical operations at risk of disruption. Accordingly, we have designated information security as a governmentwide high-risk area since 1997,[3] a designation that remains in force today.[4]

Recognizing the importance of securing federal agencies' information systems, Congress enacted the Federal Information Security Management Act (FISMA) in December 2002 to strengthen the security of information and systems within federal agencies.[5] FISMA requires each agency to develop, document, and implement an agencywide information security program for the information and systems that support the operations and assets of the agency, using a risk-based approach to information security management. Such a program includes assessing risks; developing and implementing security plans, policies, and procedures; providing security awareness and specialized training; testing and evaluating the effectiveness of controls; planning, implementing, evaluating, and documenting remedial actions to address information security deficiencies; and ensuring continuity of operations.

The BSA and FinCEN

The BSA, enacted by Congress in 1970, authorizes the Secretary of the Treasury to issue regulations requiring financial institutions to retain records and file reports useful in criminal, tax, and regulatory investigations. Following the September 11, 2001, terrorist attacks, Congress passed the USA PATRIOT Act, which, among other things, amended the BSA to expand the number of industries subject to BSA regulation and required financial institutions to establish proactive anti-money laundering programs to combat terrorist financing.[6] In addition, the USA PATRIOT Act expanded reporting requirements and allowed the records and reports collected under the BSA to be used in the conduct of intelligence or counterintelligence activities to protect against international terrorism.

As the administrator of the BSA, FinCEN, a bureau within Treasury, is tasked with the mission of safeguarding the U.S. financial system from money laundering, terrorist financing, and other abuses. In fulfilling this mission, FinCEN plays four key roles: (1) performing analysis in support of law enforcement; (2) issuing regulations and enforcing compliance; (3) facilitating information-sharing of BSA data; and (4) coordinating with foreign counterparts. Providing analysis was FinCEN's original mission when it was established in 1990, a role that it continues to perform. In its capacity as regulator, FinCEN develops regulations and delegates authority to eight other federal agencies to perform compliance examinations for BSA reporting requirements for referral to FinCEN, which retains enforcement authority. In terms of information-sharing, sections 361 and 362 of the USA PATRIOT Act mandate that FinCEN create and maintain networks to enable electronic filing of BSA reports and facilitate dissemination of the data to law enforcement and regulatory agencies. In addition, FinCEN participates in and promotes international collaboration and information-sharing among its foreign counterparts to detect and deter illicit financial activities. Between fiscal years 2002 and 2007, FinCEN's budget grew from $47.5 million to $73.2 million. According to FinCEN, this growth has taken place primarily because of the expansion of its regulatory functions.

Information That Supports FinCEN's Mission

FinCEN relies on information submitted under BSA reporting requirements to fulfill its mission. Specifically, FinCEN collects information submitted and disseminates it to law enforcement and regulatory agencies. The information primarily consists of Currency Transaction Reports and Suspicious Activity Reports that are filed by financial institutions. Currency Transaction Reports must be filed for any account cash withdrawals and deposits, currency exchanges, and wire transfers purchased with cash exceeding $10,000. Suspicious Activity Reports must be filed by financial institutions if a transaction involves or aggregates a minimum threshold[7] of funds or other assets and the institution knows, suspects, or has reason to suspect that the transaction is a violation of law. Law enforcement agencies use the information in these reports in combination with other information that they collect to link individuals and their activities, hinder activities, and prosecute criminals. Financial regulators, such as the Federal Deposit Insurance Corporation and the National Credit Union Administration, use the information to examine financial institutions for compliance with the BSA.

Currency Transaction Reports and Suspicious Activity Reports contain highly sensitive, detailed information about the financial activity of private individuals[8] that is intended to help federal, state, and local law enforcement agencies in their investigations and, thus, potentially hinder criminal activity. Inappropriate disclosure, modification, or misuse of this information could undermine the ability of the federal government, financial institutions, and law enforcement agencies to combat money laundering and terrorist financing.

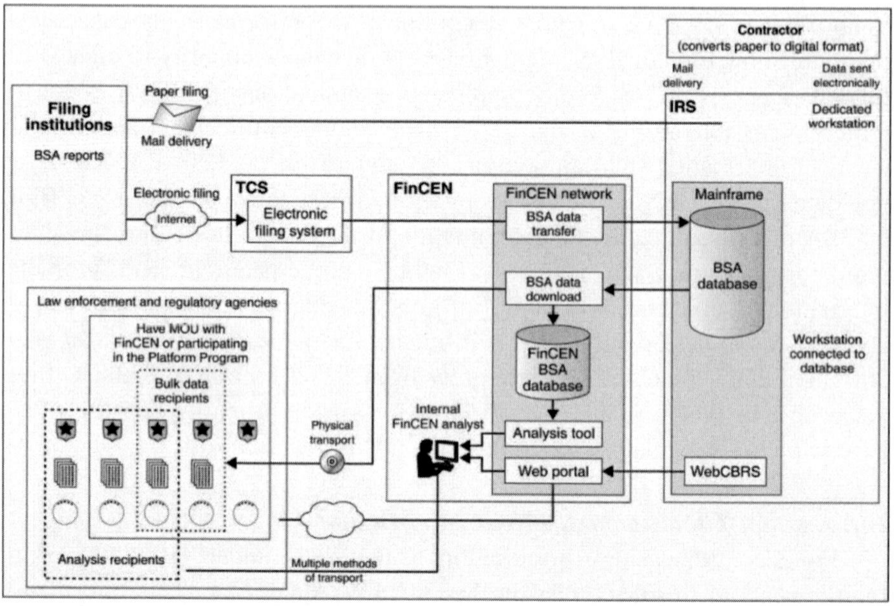

Figure 1 BSA Environment Operational Relationships and Data Flow

Information Systems That Support FinCEN's Mission

Information systems located at FinCEN, TCS, and IRS comprise the overall computing environment where BSA information is collected, processed, stored, disseminated, and protected in support of FinCEN's mission. In its own computing environment, FinCEN maintains a Web portal by which law enforcement agencies, regulatory agencies, and FinCEN employees access BSA data. It also has an analysis tool that it uses to provide analyses to law enforcement customers and a database containing a copy of the

BSA database maintained by IRS. These systems reside on FinCEN's network infrastructure. Additional systems are operated at TCS, including the electronic filing system and the supporting TCS network infrastructure. FinCEN's electronic filing system is operated on the TCS network under a hosting agreement. FinCEN also relies on systems operated by IRS, including the BSA database and the Web-based Currency Banking and Retrieval System (WebCBRS). WebCBRS and the database reside on a mainframe computer and supporting network infrastructure at an IRS computing facility

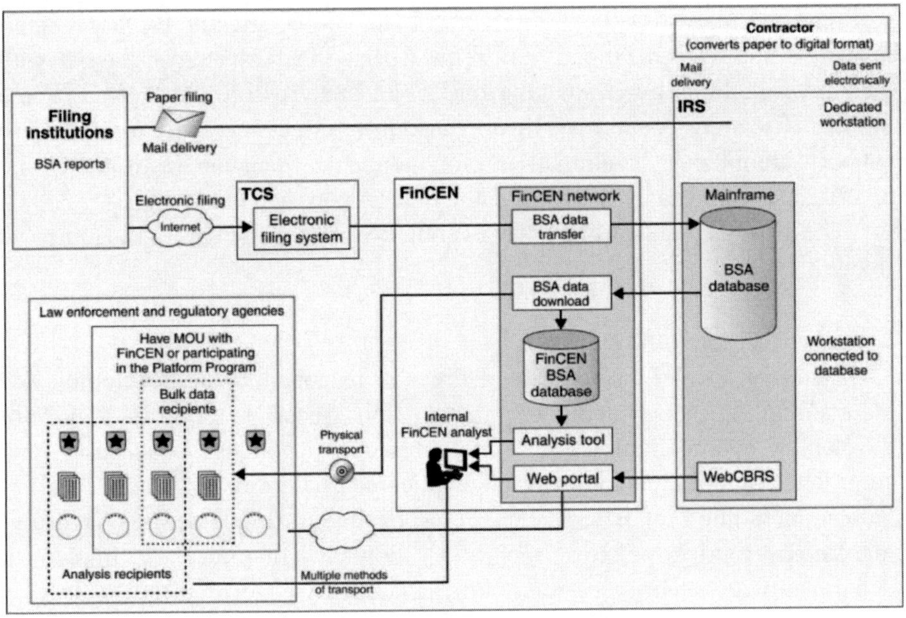

Figure 1. BSA Environment Operational Relationships and Data Flow

Information Flow in the BSA Environment

The information in BSA reports submitted by financial institutions comprise the data that is stored in the BSA database at IRS. Most reports[9] are submitted electronically, either singly or in batch form, over the Internet to the electronic filing system; FinCEN moves this data through its network infrastructure and passes them to IRS. Reports submitted in paper form are mailed directly to IRS; they are then forwarded to a contractor, who converts the reports into digital format and returns them electronically. IRS personnel then manually upload the data to the database.

BSA data are provided to law enforcement and regulatory agencies in multiple ways. Organizations may access the data through FinCEN's Web portal, which provides access to the WebCBRS application. These organizations either have a memorandum of understanding with FinCEN, which allows them to access the portal remotely through the Internet, or participate in FinCEN's Platform Program, which allows them to access the portal on-site at FinCEN. In addition, certain federal agencies also periodically receive bulk downloads of BSA data for use at their agencies. FinCEN also has its own analysis tool that it uses to provide investigative leads to support financial criminal investigations and produce a variety of analytical products that can be used by law enforcement to more effectively target their investigations. Organizations may request that FinCEN analysts assist with their investigations by conducting queries or analyses on their behalf. Some internal IRS analysts and investigators also have direct access to WebCBRS to support compliance examinations for nonbank financial institutions and investigations of money laundering and other tax-related crime.

The flow of data through the overall BSA environment is illustrated in figure 1.

Security Responsibilities

Treasury's Chief Information Officer is responsible for developing and maintaining a departmentwide information security program and for developing and maintaining information security policies, procedures, and control techniques that address all applicable requirements. Each Treasury bureau, including FinCEN and IRS, is responsible for implementing Treasury-mandated security policies within its domain. In order to implement departmentwide security policies, FinCEN and IRS are required to develop their own information security programs, including their own security compliance functions.

In addition, the organizations operating the systems that support FinCEN's mission have formalized agreements that define security responsibilities. For example, FinCEN's hosting agreement with TCS documents security prerequisites and the responsibilities of TCS as the host network. Additionally, FinCEN and IRS have an interconnection security agreement that identifies the technical requirements of the interconnection between the FinCEN network and the IRS systems that store and process the data. The agreement specifies that FinCEN owns the data and indicates that the environment where the data resides is to be logically isolated from the other systems at IRS.

FinCEN, TCS, and IRS Had Not Fully Implemented Appropriate Security Controls and Practices to Protect Information and Systems Supporting FinCEN's Mission

Although FinCEN, TCS, and IRS had implemented many information security controls to protect the information and systems supporting FinCEN's mission, weaknesses existed in several critical areas. Specifically, the organizations did not consistently implement effective electronic access controls, including user accounts and passwords, access rights and permissions, encryption of sensitive data, protection of information system boundaries, audit and monitoring of security-relevant events, and physical security to prevent, limit, and detect access to their critical financial and sensitive systems. In addition, weaknesses in other information system controls, including managing system configurations, patching sensitive systems, and service continuity, further increase the risk to the information and systems that support FinCEN's mission. One key reason for these weaknesses was that FinCEN and IRS had not yet fully implemented key elements of their information security programs. As a result, BSA data—containing highly sensitive personal and financial information about private individuals that is used by the law enforcement community to identify and prosecute illegal activity—are at an increased risk of unauthorized use, modification, or disclosure.

Some Access Controls Had Been Implemented, but Significant Weaknesses Remained

A basic management objective for any organization is to protect the resources that support its critical operations from unauthorized access. Organizations accomplish this objective by designing and implementing controls that are intended to prevent, limit, and detect unauthorized access to computing resources, programs, information, and facilities. Inadequate access controls diminish the reliability of computerized information and increase the risk of unauthorized disclosure, modification, and destruction of sensitive information and disruption of service. Access controls include those related to (1) user identification and authentication, (2) authorization, (3) cryptography, (4) boundary protection, (5) audit and monitoring, and (6) physical security.

Weaknesses in each of these areas existed across the BSA environment, as the following sections in this report demonstrate.

Policies for Identifying and Authenticating Users Were Established, but Were Not Always Consistently Implemented

A computer system must be able to identify and authenticate different users so that activities on the system can be linked to specific individuals. When an organization assigns unique user accounts to specific users, the system is able to distinguish one user from another—a process called identification. The system must also establish the validity of a user's claimed identity by requesting some kind of information, such as a password, that is known only by the user—a process known as authentication. FinCEN policy states that user IDs and passwords should not be shared. National Institute of Standards and Technology (NIST) guidance states that information systems should prohibit passwords from being reused for a specified number of generations and that complex passwords reduce the risk that a password could be guessed by an attacker. IRS requires that passwords not be shared, that each account have a unique user ID, and that default mainframe passwords be changed when information systems are installed.

Weaknesses in identification and authentication controls existed over the information and systems supporting FinCEN's mission at FinCEN, TCS, and IRS, including the following:

- Although FinCEN had established policies for identifying and authenticating users and required complex passwords on its databases, it allowed multiple users to share an account on the dedicated workstation used to download BSA data from IRS.
- TCS also had not consistently implemented effective password controls. For example, three accounts on a key database, including an administrative account, had passwords that were not complex, making them easily guessable. Additionally, the electronic filing application did not lock out user accounts after a specific number of unsuccessful log-in attempts.
- IRS did not always effectively control user identification and authentication. For example, it did not change easily guessable default passwords for two special purpose accounts that provided interactive mainframe privileges, access to BSA data, and powerful processing capabilities.

As a result of these weaknesses, there is an increased risk that malicious individuals could gain inappropriate access to sensitive BSA applications and data.

User Access to Sensitive Data Was Not Always Appropriately Authorized

Authorization is the process of granting or denying access rights and privileges to a protected resource, such as a network, system, application, function, or file. A key component of authorization and a basic principle for securing computer resources and data is the concept of least privilege. Least privilege means that users are granted access to only those programs and files that they need in order to perform their official duties. To restrict legitimate users' access in this way, organizations establish access rights and permissions. User rights are allowable actions that can be assigned to users or to groups of users. File and directory permissions are rules that regulate which users have access to a particular file or directory and the extent of that access. To avoid unintentionally giving users unnecessary access to sensitive files, directories, and special machine instructions that programs use to communicate with the operating system, an organization must give careful consideration to its assignment of rights and permissions.

FinCEN requires that access to resources be given only to users who need it, that managers re-evaluate the system privileges granted to users at least once every 6 months, and that all system privileges and access to information immediately cease when employees leave the organization. Additionally, IRS requires that information systems uniquely identify users that access sensitive information and that such access be given only to those employees with a valid need to know.

Weaknesses in authorization controls existed at FinCEN and TCS that could place the information and systems that support FinCEN's mission at risk, as the following examples indicate:

- FinCEN did not always adequately restrict access to sensitive files. The bureau had assigned rights and permissions to network users; however, it did not consistently protect all network resources. For example, it assigned excessive permissions to a shared network drive that stored BSA data received from IRS. In addition, FinCEN managers did not re-evaluate user privileges every 6 months. Further, two former employees retained access to the Web portal for at least 2 weeks after they left FinCEN.

- Additionally, TCS did not consistently ensure that access to resources was appropriate. For example, it did not restrict access to log files and other operating system files associated with the electronic filing application to only those who needed the access to perform their jobs, increasing the risk that data could be accessed by unauthorized users or that malicious activity could potentially go undetected. In addition, it allowed users direct access to a shared administrative account, making it difficult to establish individual accountability for privileged activities.

  More serious authorization control weaknesses existed over the information and systems supporting FinCEN's mission operated by IRS, including the following:
- IRS did not implement controls to restrict access to data and systems to only those who needed it. IRS and FinCEN created a memorandum of understanding and an interconnection security agreement in which IRS agreed to secure the systems and data supporting FinCEN by isolating them from other systems and controlling IRS user access to the systems and data through a dedicated network. However, IRS did not isolate the systems and data from its other systems and had not restricted user access to the systems and data via a dedicated network. Instead, other paths allowed any of its employees to gain access without detection, most of whom did not have a legitimate need for such access:
  - IRS allowed more than 600 IRS employees to have privileges on the mainframe supporting FinCEN's mission that they did not need in order to do their jobs; the privileges allowed them to interactively enter commands into the system and perform activities that are usually associated with programming and system administration.
  - Mainframe files had excessive permissions that could allow their contents to be read or copied by any user able to gain interactive access to the mainframe.
  - The systems supporting FinCEN's mission shared their data storage devices with other IRS systems, allowing users with interactive access to the mainframe the ability to view information about the BSA related datasets, including their location, even though most of them did not have a job-related need for this information.
  - Additionally, IRS did not maintain documentation of approved access privileges allowed to each system resource by each user

group on its systems supporting FinCEN's mission, limiting IRS's ability to monitor and verify access privileges.

By allowing access to information and systems to individuals who do not have a legitimate job-related need, FinCEN, TCS, and IRS are placing these data and systems at increased risk of unauthorized access or disclosure, which could hinder FinCEN's ability to fulfill its mission.

FinCEN Employed Encryption, but Sensitive Data Were Not Always Adequately Protected

Cryptography[10] underlies many of the mechanisms used to enforce the confidentiality and integrity of critical and sensitive information. One primary principle of cryptography is encryption. Encryption can be used to provide basic confidentiality and integrity for data by transforming plain text into cipher text using a special value known as a key and a mathematical process known as an algorithm. FinCEN requires that sensitive information must be encrypted when it is transmitted or stored. In addition, IRS requires the use of insecure protocols to be restricted on its systems in order to protect passwords and other sensitive data.

Weaknesses in encryption controls over the information and systems supporting FinCEN's mission at FinCEN and IRS could place sensitive data at risk, as the following examples indicate:

- Although FinCEN employed encryption mechanisms to protect data on its network and workstations, not all sensitive data were encrypted. FinCEN employed software to encrypt data on removable flash drives. However, user IDs and passwords for a key system were transmitted unencrypted across the FinCEN network, making them vulnerable to being compromised and used to gain unauthorized access. Additionally, although FinCEN encrypted the hard drives on its laptop computers, the encryption software did not protect data after the computers had been booted to a running state.
- IRS did not always secure the transmission of information on its network. For example, user IDs and passwords for the mainframe were transmitted unencrypted over the network, making them vulnerable to being compromised. In addition, it did not use certificates to ensure that the encrypted communications path between its network and the BSA database could be trusted.

As a result, weaknesses in encryption increased the risk of exposing data at FinCEN and IRS to unnecessary disclosure or misuse by unauthorized individuals.

FinCEN and TCS Implemented Boundary Protection and Intrusion Detection Controls, but Weaknesses Remained

Boundary protections demarcate logical or physical boundaries between unknown users and protected information and systems. Best practices dictate that organizations allocate publicly accessible information system components to separate subnetworks with separate physical network interfaces and that key components within private networks are also adequately segregated as subnetworks. Unnecessary connectivity to an organization's network increases not only the number of access paths that must be managed and the complexity of the task, but also the risk of unauthorized access in a shared environment. NIST guidance states that information systems should establish a trusted communications path between remote users, that firewalls should control both outgoing and incoming network traffic, and that boundary mechanisms separate computing systems and network infrastructures. In addition, IRS requires that test and production environments be kept separate.

Although FinCEN and TCS had employed controls to segregate sensitive areas of their networks and protect them from intrusion, the organizations did not always adequately control the logical and physical boundaries protecting information and systems supporting FinCEN's mission, as the following examples indicate:

- FinCEN had not fully implemented controls to protect the boundaries of its network. For example, FinCEN did not configure its virtual private network[11] with controls to validate whether the systems that connected to it were secure. In addition, it did not employ host-based firewalls on its workstations.
- TCS also did not always control the logical and physical boundaries protecting the systems supporting FinCEN. For example, TCS stored sensitive files on a network segment that was less secure than other segments. In addition, the TCS e-mail server allowed spoofed e-mail messages[12] and potentially harmful attachments to be delivered to FinCEN.
- IRS did not restrict the processing of sensitive data on its systems that support FinCEN. For example, updates to libraries containing key control programs and source code and creation and deletion of

datasets containing BSA information were submitted from areas of the mainframe that did not support FinCEN. In addition, some of this processing originated from a test environment.

As a result, there is an increased risk that individuals, internal and external to FinCEN, TCS, and IRS, could gain unauthorized access to the information and systems that support FinCEN's mission.

Audit and Monitoring Controls Were Implemented, but They Did Not Always Capture Key Events

To establish individual accountability, monitor compliance with security policies, and investigate security violations, it is crucial to determine what, when, and by whom specific actions have been taken on a system. Organizations accomplish this by implementing system or security software that provides an audit trail of needed information in the desired format and locations so they can use it to determine the source of a transaction or attempted transaction and to monitor users' activities. The way in which organizations configure system or security software determines the nature and extent of information that the audit trails can provide. A key aspect of this process is managing audit logs.[13] Organizations should periodically review audit log design, review processes and procedures, and implement changes as needed to ensure that logs effectively detect security incidents.

FinCEN requires audit logs to be maintained for all information systems and for unsuccessful log-in attempts to be recorded; in addition, it requires intrusion detection systems[14] to be employed to protect the network from external threats. Similarly, IRS policy requires that audit records be created, protected, and retained to enable the monitoring, analysis, investigation, and reporting of unlawful, unauthorized, or inappropriate information system activity.

Weaknesses in audit and monitoring controls existed over the systems supporting FinCEN's mission at FinCEN and IRS, including the following:

- FinCEN logged user activity for two key applications; however, it did not always log security events on its databases. For example, the bureau did not enable auditing on the FinCEN BSA database and did not log failed log-in attempts to the database's error logs. In addition, its intrusion detection systems did not capture data from complete sessions or inspect outbound encrypted traffic.

- IRS did not effectively capture changes to datasets on its mainframe. Specifically, it did not configure its security software to log successful changes to key datasets that contain parameters and procedures used to support production operations of the operating system, system utilities, and user applications, including WebCBRS.

As a result of weaknesses in logging and monitoring controls at FinCEN and IRS, there is an increased risk that unauthorized activity would not be effectively detected or investigated.

FinCEN Controlled Physical Access to Sensitive Areas, but Did Not Control Laptop Computers Entering and Exiting Its Facility

Physical security controls are important for protecting computer facilities and resources from espionage, sabotage, damage, and theft. These controls restrict physical access to computer resources, usually by limiting access to the buildings and rooms in which the resources are housed and by periodically reviewing the access granted in order to ensure that it continues to be appropriate. FinCEN's physical security policy requires that access to sensitive areas be restricted to authorized personnel and that all information system-related items, including laptop computers, are to be monitored and controlled when they enter or leave FinCEN.

Although FinCEN controlled access to sensitive areas, it did not always implement a physical security control. FinCEN implemented an electronic badging system to control access to sensitive areas. However, at the time of our site visits, security guards at the FinCEN facility did not inspect laptop computers entering and exiting the facility. Controlling the entry and exit of laptop computers would reduce the risk that a malicious individual could introduce malware onto the FinCEN network or that sensitive data could be taken off site without authorization.

Other Information Security Weaknesses Existed

In addition to access controls, other important controls should be in place to protect the confidentiality, integrity, and availability of an organization's information. These controls include policies, procedures, and techniques for (1) ensuring continuity of computer processing operations in the event of a disaster or unexpected interruption; (2) securely configuring information systems and preventing unauthorized changes to systems; and (3) protecting systems from known vulnerabilities. Weaknesses in these control areas increased the risk of unauthorized use, disclosure, modification, or loss of sensitive information and information systems supporting FinCEN's mission.

FinCEN Documented Contingency Plans for Major Systems, but the Plans for High-Risk Systems Were Not Fully Tested

Continuity of operations planning, which includes contingency planning, is a critical component of information protection. Continuity planning controls should be designed to ensure that when unexpected events occur, critical operations continue without interruption or are promptly resumed and that critical and sensitive data are protected. These controls include (1) environmental controls and procedures designed to protect information resources and minimize the risk of unplanned interruptions and (2) a well-tested plan to recover critical operations should interruptions occur. If service continuity controls are inadequate, even relatively minor interruptions can result in lost or incorrectly processed data, which can cause financial losses, expensive recovery efforts, and inaccurate or incomplete financial or management information. NIST guidance states that contingency plans for high-risk systems should be tested at an alternate processing site. In addition, FinCEN policy requires contingency plans to be documented for each major system and tested at least annually.

FinCEN documented and tested contingency plans for each of the three major systems we reviewed, including two high-risk systems. For the high-risk systems, the plan for the network infrastructure had been tested with a table top exercise, and portions of the Web portal plan had been simulated in a functional exercise. Although the plans had not undergone a full functional test at FinCEN's alternate processing site, the bureau identified this as a weakness and planned to conduct tests at the alternate site once the infrastructure at the site was capable of supporting a full test. However, until FinCEN tests the plans at the alternate site, the risk that FinCEN may not be able to effectively recover these systems and resume normal operations after a disruption is increased.

IRS and FinCEN Implemented Configuration Management and System Change Controls, but Weaknesses Remained

The purpose of configuration management is to establish and maintain the integrity of an organization's systems. Organizations can better ensure that only authorized applications and programs are placed into operation by establishing and maintaining baseline configurations and by monitoring changes to these configurations. Organizations should ensure that changes to systems are necessary, work as intended, and do not result in the loss of data or program integrity by documenting, authorizing, testing, and independently reviewing changes. FinCEN's configuration management policy requires that change control procedures be developed and that documentation be created and retained for configuration changes. Additionally, NIST guidance states that change control procedures should address emergency changes. Further, IRS policy requires the establishment and maintenance of baseline configurations and inventories of organizational information systems and the establishment and enforcement of security configuration settings for IT products employed in organizational information systems.

Weaknesses existed in configuration management controls at FinCEN and IRS over the systems that support FinCEN's mission, including the following:

- FinCEN maintained an inventory for its network assets, established configuration management plans for its major systems, and established processes for documenting, authorizing, testing, and reviewing system changes. However, its configuration management plans were not fully documented and not all system changes included required documentation. For example, the Web portal plan did not describe the documentation that was required for system changes and the electronic filing system plan did not describe a key step in the change control process. In addition, the Web portal and network infrastructure plans did not include procedures for handling emergency changes. Moreover, although its network infrastructure configuration management plan required security assessments to be documented for changes, FinCEN did not document them for any of the eight infrastructure changes we reviewed.
- IRS did not always adequately manage the configuration of sensitive systems. IRS had adequately documented and tested the seven changes to the WebCBRS application that we reviewed. However, IRS did not maintain or enforce a baseline configuration on the mainframe system that supports the WebCBRS system and the BSA database, as well as other critical IRS systems.

Until FinCEN fully documents change control procedures and system changes, there is an increased risk that changes to its systems could be unnecessary, may not work as intended, or may result in the unintentional loss of data or program integrity. Moreover, without a baseline configuration, IRS is unable to adequately track and monitor changes to its mainframe, potentially placing sensitive BSA data at risk.

FinCEN Established a Patch Management Program, but Key Systems Were Missing Critical Patches

Patch management is a critical process that can help alleviate many of the challenges of securing computing systems.[15] As vulnerabilities in a system are discovered, attackers may attempt to exploit them, possibly causing significant damage. Malicious acts can range from defacing Web sites to taking control of entire systems, thereby being able to read, modify, or delete sensitive information; disrupt operations; or launch attacks against other organizations' systems. After a vulnerability is validated, the software vendor may develop and test a patch or workaround to mitigate the vulnerability. Incident response groups and software vendors issue information updates on the vulnerability and the availability of patches. FinCEN policy requires all of its systems to be patched on a monthly basis, that patches be tested on nonproduction systems before being loaded onto production systems, and a log be maintained of all patches applied to each system.

FinCEN did not always apply patches in a timely manner, and sensitive systems were missing critical patches. Although the bureau required all of its systems to be patched monthly, it was only applying patches to the Web portal application every 3 months. Furthermore, several systems that processed BSA data were missing critical patches or were running software that was out of date. Because the organization was not always applying patches in a timely manner, had not yet installed many critical patches, and had not upgraded software on all of its systems, data were unnecessarily vulnerable to compromise.

FinCEN and IRS had not Fully Implemented Elements of their Information Security Programs

A key reason for the information security weaknesses over the information and systems supporting FinCEN's mission is that FinCEN and IRS had not fully implemented information security program elements required by FISMA. FISMA requires agencies to develop, document, and implement an information security program that, among other things, includes

- periodic assessments of the risk and magnitude of harm that could result from the unauthorized access, use, disclosure, disruption, modification, or destruction of information and information systems;
- policies and procedures that (1) are based on risk assessments, (2) cost-effectively reduce information security risks to an acceptable level, (3) ensure that information security is addressed throughout the life cycle of each system, and (4) ensure compliance with applicable requirements;
- plans for providing adequate information security for networks, facilities, and systems;
- security awareness training to inform personnel of information security risks and of their responsibilities in complying with agency policies and procedures, as well as training personnel with significant security responsibilities for information security;
- periodic testing and evaluation of the effectiveness of information security policies, procedures, and practices, to be performed with a frequency depending on risk, but no less than annually, and that includes testing of management, operational, and technical controls for every system identified in the agency's required inventory of major information systems; and
- a process for planning, implementing, evaluating, and documenting remedial action to address any deficiencies in its information security policies, procedures, or practices.

Although FinCEN made progress in implementing its information security program, it had not yet fully implemented key activities. Additionally, although we did not fully evaluate IRS's security program separately as a part of this review, in previous reports we have found that key elements of IRS's program have shortcomings. Until all key elements of its information security programs are fully and consistently implemented, FinCEN and IRS will not have sufficient assurance that new weaknesses will not emerge and that sensitive data and systems are adequately safeguarded from inadvertent or deliberate misuse, fraudulent use, improper disclosure, or destruction.[16]

FinCEN Conducted Risk Assessments for Systems Transmitting and Storing BSA Data

Identifying and assessing information security risks are essential steps in determining what controls are required to mitigate the risks. Moreover, by increasing awareness of risks, these assessments can generate support for the policies and controls that are adopted in order to help ensure that these policies and controls operate as intended. NIST guidelines state that the identification of risk for an information technology system requires an understanding of the system's processing environment, including data and information, system and data criticality, and system and data sensitivity. Furthermore, according to NIST, risk management should identify threats and vulnerabilities, set priorities for actions to reduce risks, identify new controls or countermeasures, and determine risks remaining after implementing the new control, also known as residual risk. FinCEN risk assessment policy requires that risk assessments be documented for all systems, conducted in accordance with NIST guidance, and updated at least every 3 years as part of the certification and accreditation process.

FinCEN documented risk assessments for all three of the major systems we reviewed; they were conducted in accordance with FinCEN policy and NIST guidance for risk assessments. The assessments were current, documented potential threats, and recommended corrective actions for mitigating or eliminating the vulnerabilities identified.

FinCEN Made Progress Toward Developing and Documenting Information Security Policies and Procedures, but Lacked Detailed Implementing Guidance

A key element of an effective information security program is establishing and implementing appropriate policies, procedures, and technical standards to govern security over an agency's computing environment. Moreover, such policies and procedures should integrate all security aspects of an organization's interconnected environment, including local and wide area networks and interconnections to contractors and other federal agencies that support critical mission operations. Establishing and documenting security policies is important because they are the primary mechanism by which management communicates its views and requirements; these policies also serve as the basis for adopting specific procedures and technical controls. In addition, agencies need to take the actions necessary to effectively implement or execute these procedures and controls. Otherwise, agency systems and information will not receive the protection that should be provided by the security policies and procedures.

Although FinCEN had made progress toward developing and documenting information security policies and procedures, the policies did not always include key information, and detailed implementing guidance for its policies did not always exist. FinCEN updated its policies and approved them in June 2008; the policies replaced older ones that had not been updated since 2003. However, shortcomings in the updated policies existed. For example, although FinCEN established a patch management policy, the implementing guidance for UNIX patches did not address prioritization of critical patches. In addition, its policy requiring that the network be protected by an intrusion detection system did not require that outbound network traffic be inspected. Further, the bureau did not have detailed implementation guidance for securely configuring its virtual private network. The weaknesses we identified in each of these controls demonstrate the need for such guidance.

FinCEN and IRS Developed System Security Plans, but FinCEN Did Not Document All Required Controls

An information system security plan should provide a complete and up-to-date overview of a system's security requirements and describe the controls that are in place or planned to meet those requirements. Office of Management and Budget (OMB) Circular A-130 specifies that agencies develop and implement system security plans for major applications and for general support systems and that these plans address policies and procedures for providing management, operational, and technical controls. Under FISMA, federal agencies are required to categorize information systems as low, moderate, or high impact; apply the appropriate set of baseline security controls in accordance with NIST guidance; and document the security controls in a system security plan. In addition, NIST recommends that security plans include, among other topics, existing or planned security controls, the name of the individual responsible for the security of the system, a description of the system and its interconnected environment, and rules of behavior for individuals accessing the system.

FinCEN also requires that its system security plans describe the system's security requirements, identify the security controls and whether they are planned or implemented for a system, and that they be reviewed, updated, and reapproved by management at least annually, or whenever a significant change to the system occurs. Additionally, IRS requires that system security plans document the security controls for systems, whether planned or in place, as well as rules of behavior for individuals accessing the system.

Although FinCEN documented system security plans for each of its major information systems, it did not always consistently document controls. While the three system security plans we reviewed documented the status of almost all of the required management, operational, and technical controls, two plans for systems categorized as high impact did not document five required security controls. During our review, FinCEN provided updated versions of the plans; however, one of them still did not document one control or describe how another control was implemented.

IRS documented system security plans for each of its three major systems that support FinCEN's mission. The plans included information required by OMB; documented the management, operational, and technical controls in place; and mapped the controls directly to those prescribed by NIST.

FinCEN Employees Completed Security Awareness Training

An important component of an information security program is providing required training so that users understand system security risks and their own role in implementing related policies and controls to mitigate those risks. FISMA mandates that federal employees and contractors who use agency information systems be provided with periodic training in information security awareness. FISMA also requires agencies to provide appropriate training on information security to personnel who have significant security responsibilities. This training, described in NIST guidance,[17] should inform personnel, including contractors and other users of information systems supporting the operations and assets of an agency, of information security risks associated with their activities and their roles and responsibilities to properly and effectively implement the practices that are designed to reduce these risks. Depending on an employee's specific security role, training could include specialized topics, such as incident detection and response, physical security, or firewall configuration. FinCEN also requires all of its employees and contractors to complete annual security awareness training and for individuals with significant security responsibilities to complete specialized security awareness training annually.

FinCEN implemented a security awareness training program and ensured that its employees and contractors completed it annually. The annual training given to all employees and contractors included topics that were consistent with NIST guidance, such as laws and regulations, e-mail security, procedures for handling sensitive information, and security threats such as viruses. The bureau reported that all of its 471 employees and contractors who were required to do so completed the training between June 2007 and July 2008. FinCEN provided certificates documenting that all 17 of the employees that we selected had completed required training and that all 8 of the employees holding significant IT responsibilities that we selected had completed the required specialized training.

FinCEN Conducted Periodic Vulnerability Scans, but the Scans Were Not Always Comprehensive or Timely

An important element of an information security program is ongoing testing and evaluation to ensure that systems are in compliance with policies and controls that are both appropriate and effective. This type of oversight is a fundamental element because it demonstrates management's commitment to the security program, reminds employees of their roles and responsibilities, and identifies and mitigates areas of noncompliance and ineffectiveness. Although control tests and evaluations may encourage compliance with security policies, the full benefits of such activities will not be achieved unless the results improve the security program. Analyzing the results of monitoring efforts—as well as security reviews performed by external audit organizations—provides security specialists and business managers with a means of identifying new problem areas, reassessing the appropriateness of existing controls, and identifying the need for new controls. NIST requires organizations to scan information systems for vulnerabilities; in addition, it states that vulnerability analysis for custom software and applications includes specialized approaches such as review of source code. In addition, according to commercial vendors, running scanning software in an authenticated mode allows the software to detect additional vulnerabilities. FinCEN policy also requires periodic scanning of its systems every 3 months to detect potential vulnerabilities.

Although FinCEN conducted periodic vulnerability scans of major systems, the scans were not always comprehensive or timely. FinCEN scanned its workstations and network infrastructure, but did not scan databases or applications; it also did not scan or conduct independent reviews of source code for its internally developed applications. Further, scanning had not been conducted quarterly; in June 2008, FinCEN officials told us that they had not conducted any scans since February 2008, a period of 4 months. As a result, FinCEN could be unaware of many undetected vulnerabilities in its applications, systems, and network in a timely manner.

FinCEN Improved Its Process for Verifying Corrective Actions, but IRS's Corrective Actions Were Not Always Effective

In its guidance to agencies, OMB requires agencies to develop remedial action plans, also known as plans of action and milestones. A remedial action plan assists agencies in the identification, assessment, prioritization, and monitoring of the progress of corrective efforts for weaknesses found in systems and programs. FinCEN policy requires that the agency track vulnerabilities found during security assessments, together with planned and implemented mitigation actions to correct these weaknesses, in each system's respective remedial action plan. IRS has a similar policy, which requires that it track the status of resolution for all weaknesses and verify that each weakness is corrected.

FinCEN developed a new remedial action management process to manage and mitigate security weaknesses in its systems. FinCEN officials told us that the bureau did not have a process to document and validate remedial actions prior to March 2008 and that the new process was developed in order to address this. The process describes how the bureau plans to identify, prioritize, and track vulnerabilities as they are addressed. Among other things, the new process requires

- monthly meetings between key staff and the Information Security System Officer in order to review the status of new and existing vulnerabilities;
- vulnerabilities to be prioritized according to risk; and
- all information concerning remedial actions to be updated at least monthly.

FinCEN officials told us that they had collected supporting documentation when remedial actions were completed and provided us with examples. However, FinCEN's procedure for the new process did not specify that supporting documentation was required. Requiring supporting documentation in the procedure would better ensure that remedial actions are verified as effective.

As we have previously reported,[18] IRS's verification process for determining whether remedial actions were implemented was not always effective. In January 2009, we reported that IRS indicated that it had corrected or mitigated 65 previously reported weaknesses but that 16 still existed at the time of our review; 3 of these weaknesses affect the systems that support FinCEN's mission. We have identified a similar weakness in both our January 2008[19] and March 2007[20] reports; however, this condition continues to exist. Without a sound remediation process, IRS will not have assurance that the proper resources will be applied to known vulnerabilities or that those vulnerabilities will be properly mitigated. We have previously recommended that IRS implement a revised remedial action verification process that ensures actions are fully implemented.

CONCLUSIONS

FinCEN, TCS, and IRS have taken important steps in implementing numerous controls to protect the information and systems that support FinCEN's mission. However, significant weaknesses in access controls and other information security controls existed at all three organizations that impaired their ability to ensure the confidentiality, integrity, and availability of the information and systems. FinCEN had made important progress in implementing its information security program; however, one key reason for many of the weaknesses was that FinCEN and IRS had not yet fully implemented elements of their information security programs. Further actions are needed to address the risk to the information and systems. Until (1) the organizations act to mitigate identified weaknesses and (2) FinCEN and IRS fully implement their information security programs, there is an increased risk that sensitive BSA information will not be adequately protected against unauthorized disclosure or modification and that systems could be disrupted.

RECOMMENDATIONS FOR EXECUTIVE ACTION

To better ensure the security of the overall BSA environment, we are recommending that the Secretary of the Treasury direct the Director of FinCEN to fully implement its information security program by taking the following five actions:

- Update information security policies and procedures to address key missing information such as patch prioritization and inspection of outbound network traffic, as well as to include detailed implementation guidance for issues such as securely configuring the virtual private network.
- Ensure that system security plans document all required controls and describe how all required controls are implemented.
- Conduct vulnerability scans on databases, applications, and network infrastructure on a quarterly schedule.
- Implement vulnerability scanning of custom source code or manual source code reviews.
- Update remedial action procedures to require that supporting documentation be provided to verify that corrective actions are fully implemented and effective.

In a separate report designated "Limited Official Use Only", we are making 88 detailed recommendations to the Secretary of the Treasury to strengthen information security controls at FinCEN, TCS, and IRS over the systems supporting FinCEN's mission.

AGENCY COMMENTS

In providing written comments (reprinted in app. II) on a draft of this report, Treasury's Deputy Assistant Secretary for Information Systems and Chief Information Officer stated that the department is committed to promoting the nation's security through strengthened financial systems and promoting safer and more transparent U.S. and international financial systems, noting that securely maintaining BSA information significantly contributes to this goal. He also stated that Treasury will provide a detailed corrective action plan for each of the recommendations and that many of the actions required to address the recommendations are already completed or under way.

We are sending copies of this report to interested congressional committees, the Secretary of the Treasury, the Director of FinCEN, the Commissioner of Internal Revenue, the Treasury Inspector General, and the Treasury Inspector General for Tax Administration. In addition, the report will be available at no charge on the GAO Web site at http://www.gao.gov .

If you or your staffs have any questions regarding this report, please contact Nancy Kingsbury at (202) 512-2700 or Gregory C. Wilshusen at (202) 512-6244. We can also be reached by e-mail at kingsburyn@gao.gov *and* wilshuseng@gao.gov. Contact points for our Offices of Congressional Relations and Public Affairs may be found on the last page of this report. Key contributors to this report are listed in appendix III.

Nancy R. Kingsbury
Managing Director, Applied Research and Methods

Gregory C. Wilshusen
Director, Information Security Issues

End Notes

[1] Bank Secrecy Act, Titles I and II of Pub. L. No. 91-508, 84 Stat. 1114 (1970), as amended, codified at 12 U.S.C. §§ 1829b, 1951-1959, and 31 U.S.C. §§ 5311-5322.

[2] Information security controls include access controls, configuration management, patch management, and continuity of operations. These controls are designed to ensure that access to data is appropriately restricted, that systems are configured appropriately, that systems are protected against known vulnerabilities, and that back-up and recovery plans are adequate to ensure the continuity of essential operations.

[3] GAO, *High-Risk Series: Information Management and Technology*,GAO/HR-97-9 (Washington, D.C.: February 1997).

[4] GAO, *High-Risk Series: An Update,* GAO-09-271 (Washington, D.C.: January 2009).

[5] FISMA was enacted as Title III, E-Government Act of 2002, Pub. L. No. 107-347, 116 Stat. 2946 (Dec. 17, 2002).

[6] USA PATRIOT Act, Pub. L. No. 107-56, 115 Stat. 272 (Oct. 26, 2001).

[7] 31 U.S.C. § 5318(g)(1) and 31 C.F.R. §§ 103.15–103.21. Depending on the type of financial institution, the threshold amount may vary. For example, money services businesses generally must file a Suspicious Activity Report if a transaction involves or aggregates $2,000 in funds or other assets. Suspicious Activity Report forms must be filed for certain suspicious transactions involving possible violations of law or regulation, including transactions that are broken up for the purpose of evading the BSA reporting and record-keeping requirements.

[8] In addition to the dollar amount of the cash transaction, these reports may record other sensitive information, including the name of the account owner; the name of the person actually conducting the transaction (if not the account holder); social security numbers; driver's license or identification numbers; and account numbers.

[9] According to FinCEN, approximately 71 percent of BSA submissions are made through the electronic filing system.

[10] Cryptography is the discipline that embodies principles, means, and methods for providing information security, including confidentiality, data integrity, nonrepudiation, and authenticity.

[11] A virtual private network is a private network that is maintained across a shared or public network, such as the Internet, by means of specialized security procedures. Virtual private networks are intended to provide secure connections between remote clients, such as branch offices or traveling personnel, and a central office.

[12] E-mail spoofing occurs when a user receives e-mail that appears to have originated from one source when it actually was sent from another source. E-mail spoofing is often an attempt to trick the user into making a damaging statement or releasing sensitive information (such as passwords).

[13] Log management is the process for generating, transmitting, storing, analyzing, and disposing of log data.

[14] An intrusion detection system detects inappropriate, incorrect, or anomalous activity that is aimed at disrupting the confidentiality, availability, or integrity of a protected network and its computer systems.

[15] For example, see GAO, *Information Security: Continued Action Needed to Improve Software Patch Management*, GAO-04-706 (Washington, D.C.: June 2, 2004).

[16] The information and systems at TCS that support FinCEN's mission are subject to the information security program for Treasury; however, we did not evaluate Treasury's program as part of this review.

[17] NIST, *Information Technology Security Training Requirements: A Role- and Performance-Based Model*, SP 800-16 (Gaithersburg, Md., April 1998); and NIST, *Building an*

Information Technology Security Awareness and Training Program, SP 800-50 (Gaithersburg, Md., October 2003).

[18] GAO, *Information Security: Continued Efforts Needed to Address Significant Weaknesses at IRS,* GAO-09-136 (Washington, D.C.: Jan. 9, 2009).

[19] GAO, *Information Security: IRS Needs to Address Pervasive Weaknesse,*GAO-08-211 (Washington, D.C.: Jan. 8, 2008).

[20] GAO, *Information Security: Further Efforts Needed to Address Significant Weaknesses at the Internal Revenue Service*, GAO-07-364 (Washington, D.C.: Mar. 30, 2007).

APPENDIX I: OBJECTIVE, SCOPE, AND METHODOLOGY

The objective of our review was to determine whether information security controls have been implemented that effectively protect the confidentiality, integrity, and availability of the information and information systems supporting the mission of the Financial Crimes Enforcement Network (FinCEN).

To accomplish this, we tested the effectiveness of information security and information technology-based internal controls. We focused our evaluation on the controls for the applications, databases, and network infrastructure that directly or indirectly support the processing and storage of Bank Secrecy Act (BSA) data on behalf of FinCEN at the Department of the Treasury (Treasury), FinCEN, and the Internal Revenue Service (IRS). Specifically, we evaluated FinCEN's network infrastructure and Web portal used to access BSA data; the Web-based Currency and Banking Retrieval System (WebCBRS) and the mainframe and network infrastructure supporting it at IRS; and the electronic filing system and related network infrastructure at the Treasury Communications System (TCS).

Our evaluation was based on our *Federal Information System Controls Audit Manual*, which contains guidance for reviewing information system controls that affect the confidentiality, integrity, and availability of computerized information. We also used FinCEN, IRS, and Treasury policies and procedures to evaluate the information system controls at the organizations. Additionally, where federal requirements or guidelines were applicable, such as the Federal Information Security Management Act of 2002 (FISMA) or National Institute of Standards and Technology (NIST) guidance, we used them to assess the extent to which the organizations had complied with specific requirements.

To determine whether TCS, FinCEN, and IRS had implemented access controls, contingency planning controls, and configuration controls over the information and systems that support FinCEN, we

- evaluated and reviewed the security software password settings to determine if users were appropriately identified and authenticated and if strong password management was enforced;
- examined application and system access lists and associated documentation to determine whether users were properly authorized or had more permissions than necessary to perform their assigned job functions;
- analyzed network and system configurations to determine if access paths were adequately controlled and if sensitive data were being encrypted;
- tested and observed physical access controls and environmental controls to determine if computer facilities and resources were being protected from intentional or unintentional loss or impairment;
- evaluated and reviewed backup and recovery procedures to determine if they adequately protected key systems against service interruptions;
- examined contingency plans and test results for key FinCEN systems to determine whether those plans were adequately documented, had been updated, or had been appropriately tested;
- inspected key servers, workstations, and network infrastructure devices to determine whether critical patches had been installed or were up-to-date; and
- evaluated and reviewed change request documentation to determine if system and application changes were appropriately authorized, tested, and approved.

To assess whether FinCEN had fully implemented an information security program to ensure that controls were established and maintained for its information systems, we used the requirements of FISMA, which establish key elements for an effective agencywide information security program. To evaluate FinCEN's implementation of these key elements, we

- analyzed risk assessments for key FinCEN systems to determine whether risks and threats were documented;
- examined security plans to determine if management, operational, and technical controls were in place or planned and whether these security plans were updated;

- analyzed FinCEN policies, procedures, practices, and standards to determine their effectiveness in providing guidance to personnel responsible for securing information and information systems;
- inspected training records for personnel with significant responsibilities to determine if they received training commensurate with those responsibilities;
- analyzed test plans and test results for key FinCEN systems to determine whether management, operational, and technical controls were adequately tested at least annually and were based on risk; and
- evaluated FinCEN's process to correct weaknesses to determine whether remedial action plans complied with federal guidance.

In addition, we examined IRS's security plans for WebCBRS and the related general support systems to determine if management, operational, and technical controls were in place or planned and whether these security plans were updated.

We also interviewed key security representatives and officials responsible for information security management at FinCEN, TCS, and IRS to help determine whether information system controls were in place, adequately designed, and operating effectively. We also reviewed a previous report issued by the Treasury Inspector General's Office on FinCEN information security and previous reports from GAO on IRS information security. Our work was conducted in the Washington, D.C., metropolitan area and at FinCEN, TCS, and IRS computing facilities in Virginia and Michigan.

We conducted this performance audit from March 2008 to January 2009 in accordance with generally accepted government auditing standards. Those standards require that we plan and perform the audit to obtain sufficient, appropriate evidence to provide a reasonable basis for our findings and conclusions based on our audit objective. We believe that the evidence obtained provides a reasonable basis for our findings and conclusions based on our audit objective.

APPENDIX II: COMMENTS FROM THE DEPARTMENT OF THE TREASURY

DEPARTMENT OF THE TREASURY
WASHINGTON, D.C. 20220

JAN 16 2009

Mr. Greg Wilshusen
Director, Information Security Issues
U.S. Government Accountability Office
441 G Street N.W.
Washington, D.C. 20515

Dear Mr. Wilshusen:

Thank you for the opportunity to review and comment on the Government Accountability Office (GAO) draft reports entitled, *Information Security: Further Actions Needed to Address Risks to Bank Secrecy Act Data* (GAO-09-200SU and GAO-09-195). Treasury is committed to promoting the nation's security through strengthened financial systems and promoting safer and more transparent U.S. and international financial systems. The ability to securely maintain Bank Secrecy Act (BSA) information contributes significantly to this goal. Therefore, we appreciate GAO's efforts in reviewing BSA information security.

Although the Financial Crimes Enforcement Network (FinCEN) is the administrator of the BSA, your reports correctly note that three entities within Treasury have responsibilities associated with maintaining and safeguarding BSA information: FinCEN, the Department's Office of the Chief Information Officer (OCIO) which operates the Treasury Communications System (TCS), and the Internal Revenue Service Enterprise Computing Center in Detroit (IRS ECC-Detroit). Many of the actions required to address the recommendations are already completed or underway. Specifically, of the 41 recommendations addressed to FinCEN, 18 have already been completed; of the 21 recommendations addressed to the Department's OCIO, 12 have already been completed; and of the 11 addressed to IRS, 4 have already been completed. Treasury will provide a detailed corrective action plan for each of the recommendations with the response to the final reports.

If you have any questions, please feel free to contact Mr. Ed Roback, Associate Chief Information Officer for Cyber Security at 202-622-2593.

Sincerely,

Michael D. Duffy
Deputy Assistant Secretary for Information Systems
and Chief Information Officer

In: The Bank Secrecy Act: Information Sharing… ISBN: 978-1-60741-983-9
Editor: Leif Ekstrom

Chapter 2

BANK SECRECY ACT: FEDERAL AGENCIES SHOULD TAKE ACTION TO FURTHER IMPROVE COORDINATION AND INFORMATION-SHARING EFFORTS*

U. S. Government Accountability Office

WHY GAO DID THIS STUDY

The legislative framework for combating money laundering began with the Bank Secrecy Act (BSA) in 1970 and most recently expanded in 2001with the USA PATRIOT Act. The Financial Crimes Enforcement Network (FinCEN) administers BSA and relies on multiple federal and state agencies to ensure financial institution compliance. GAO was asked to (1) describe how BSA compliance and enforcement responsibilities are distributed, (2) describe how agencies other than FinCEN are implementing those responsibilities and evaluate their coordination efforts, and (3) evaluate how FinCEN is implementing its BSA responsibilities. Among other things, GAO reviewed legislation, past GAO and Treasury reports, and agreements and guidance from all relevant agencies; and interviewed agency, association, and financial institution officials.

WHAT GAO RECOMMENDS

GAO recommends that IRS better coordinate examination schedules with state agencies; that FinCEN, the federal financial regulators, and IRS consider developing a mechanism to regularly discuss BSA examinations and procedures across all regulators; and that the FinCEN Director facilitate communication on IRS referrals, and finalize electronic data-access MOUs with state agencies and securities and futures regulators. The federal banking regulators, SEC, CFTC, IRS, and FinCEN agreed to implement the recommendations pertaining to their agencies.

WHAT GAO FOUND

FinCEN is responsible for the administration of the BSA regulatory structure, and has delegated examination responsibility to the federal banking regulators (Board of Governors of the Federal Reserve System, Federal Deposit Insurance Corporation, Office of the Comptroller of the Currency, Office of Thrift Supervision, and National Credit Union Administration), the Securities and Exchange Commission (SEC), the Commodity Futures Trading Commission (CFTC), and the Internal Revenue Service (IRS). The federal banking regulators, SEC, CFTC, securities and futures self-regulatory organizations (SRO), and state agencies also have their own separate authorities to examine for compliance among institutions they supervise and take enforcement actions for noncompliance. FinCEN has retained enforcement authority for BSA and may take enforcement actions independently or concurrently with the regulators.

While federal agencies have enhanced their BSA compliance programs, opportunities exist to improve interagency and state examination coordination. The federal banking regulators issued an interagency examination manual; SEC, CFTC, and their respective SROs developed BSA examination modules; and FinCEN and IRS, which examines nonblank financial institutions (NBFI), issued an examination manual for money services businesses (MSB). However, IRS has not fully coordinated MSB examination schedules with the states that also examine MSBs, potentially missing opportunities to reduce duplication and leverage resources. The federal financial regulators

* This is an edited, reformatted and augmented version of a U. S. Government Accountability Office publication dated February 2009.

traditionally have different compliance approaches for their industries. With respect to BSA, multiple regulators are examining for compliance with the same legislation across industries and, for some larger holding companies, within the same institution. However, they do not have a mechanism through which all regulators discuss (without industry present) how to promote greater consistency, reduce unnecessary regulatory burden, and identify concerns across industries. Federal banking regulators reported improved transparency and coordination of enforcement actions.

While FinCEN has increased regulatory resources, provided examination support, and made advances in outreach, it could improve its informationsharing efforts. FinCEN improved its system for tracking referrals but lack of a process for communication between IRS and FinCEN for IRS referrals, coupled with IRS's limited enforcement authority, may delay timely feedback to IRS-examined institutions. FinCEN completed more information-sharing memorandums of understanding (MOU) with federal and state agencies, but did not sign its MOU with CFTC until January 2009, which limited their information-sharing efforts. Some state regulators and securities and futures regulators continue to have no electronic access to BSA data. Lack of direct access to BSA data impedes their ability to identify potential risk areas on which to focus their examinations and effectively leverage resources. FinCEN officials said they finalized a data-access template in July 2008, and had begun providing more electronic access.

ABBREVIATIONS

AML	anti-money laundering
BSA	Bank Secrecy Act of 1970
BSAAG	Bank Secrecy Act Advisory Group
CFTC	Commodity Futures Trading Commission
CIP	customer identification program
CMP	civil money penalty
CMS	Case Management System
CTR	currency transaction report
FDIC	Federal Deposit Insurance Corporation
Federal Reserve	Board of Governors of the Federal Reserve System
FFIEC	Federal Financial Institutions Examination Council
FINRA	Financial Industry Regulatory Authority
FinCEN	Financial Crimes Enforcement Network

IRS	Internal Revenue Service
Justice	Department of Justice
MOU	memorandum of understanding
MSB	money services business
NBFI	nonbank financial institution
NCUA	National Credit Union Administration
NFA	National Futures Association
OCC	Office of the Comptroller of the Currency
OCIE	Office of Compliance Inspections and Examinations
OTS	Office of Thrift Supervision
RPPD	Regulatory Policy and Programs Division
SAR	suspicious activity report
SEC	Securities and Exchange Commission
SRO	self-regulatory organization
Treasury	Department of the Treasury

February 12, 2009

The Honorable Carl Levin
Chairman
The Honorable Tom Coburn
Acting Ranking Member
Permanent Subcommittee on Investigations
Committee on Homeland Security and Governmental Affairs
United States Senate

The legislative framework for combating money laundering and other financial crimes has been built over nearly four decades. The Bank Secrecy Act of 1970 (BSA) established reporting and other anti-money laundering (AML) requirements for domestic financial institutions.[1] Due to the increased sophistication of money laundering activities and concerns about terrorist financing, Congress expanded AML legislation to cover more types of institutions involved in a broader range of financial transactions. In 2001, the enactment of the USA PATRIOT Act strengthened reporting and AML requirements for securities firms, futures firms, money services businesses (MSB), and other financial institutions.[2] The regulators discussed in this report have developed programs to review financial institutions' compliance with these reporting requirements and AML requirements.

Multiple federal and state agencies operate within the BSA framework. The Financial Crimes Enforcement Network (FinCEN), a bureau of the U.S. Department of the Treasury (Treasury), is the BSA administrator. The federal financial regulators that compose the BSA compliance framework are the federal banking regulators—the Board of Governors of the Federal Reserve System (Federal Reserve), the Federal Deposit Insurance Corporation (FDIC), the Office of the Comptroller of the Currency (OCC), the Office of Thrift Supervision (OTS), and the National Credit Union Administration (NCUA)—as well as the Securities and Exchange Commission (SEC), and the Commodity Futures Trading Commission (CFTC). The Internal Revenue Service (IRS) has examination responsibilities under BSA.[3] To different extents, four of the federal banking regulators—the Federal Reserve, FDIC, OTS, and NCUA—share compliance responsibilities, such as examinations of institutions that they oversee, with state regulators. IRS, which oversees BSA/AML compliance among some state-chartered institutions, such as MSBs, also shares responsibilities with state regulators. The self-regulatory organizations (SRO) that SEC and CFTC oversee also have BSA/AML compliance responsibilities for the activities of their members.[4] Appendix II of this report provides an overview of the missions and compliance and enforcement activities of these entities and provides information on their BSA/AML-related resources and training.

As we have reported previously, FinCEN and these agencies have responded to the challenge of increased BSA/AML responsibilities by finalizing new regulations to implement the USA PATRIOT Act and applying them to industries newer to BSA/AML efforts.[5] In addition, the federal banking regulators, FinCEN, and SEC have taken enforcement actions involving BSA/AML-related violations that resulted in large penalties. But, as BSA regulation has evolved, so have financial services firms. They generally have become fewer in number and larger—providing more and varied services and products across one or more traditional financial sectors (banking, securities, futures, and insurance).[6] The proliferation of activities across industry lines also has made it all the more important that agencies with compliance-monitoring and enforcement responsibilities coordinate with each other. Given that many regulators and SROs have responsibility for overseeing compliance with BSA, Congress has raised questions about how effectively FinCEN and these entities are coordinating their BSA/AML efforts and the general soundness of the current BSA compliance and enforcement framework.

In response to your request that we review FinCEN and other federal agencies' efforts to implement BSA, we (1) describe how BSA compliance and enforcement efforts are distributed among federal and state regulators, SROs, and FinCEN; (2) describe how federal agencies other than FinCEN are implementing their BSA activities and evaluate their coordination efforts; and (3) evaluate how FinCEN is executing its BSA responsibilities and coordinating BSA efforts among the various agencies.

To address our objectives, we reviewed relevant federal legislation and prior GAO and Treasury Inspector General reports, and conducted interviews with FinCEN, federal banking regulators, SEC, CFTC, IRS, and Department of Justice (Justice) officials. We reviewed BSA compliance and enforcement guidance from all relevant agencies, memorandums of understanding (MOU), training documentation, staffing and performance measurement data, strategic plans and annual reports, and internal documentation. We also reviewed our collaboration best practices—which encompass a set of key practices that can help agencies enhance and sustain collaborative efforts.[7] Furthermore, we interviewed officials from selected state banking agencies (based on factors such as geography and types of financial activities within their states) and SROs, and officials from associations representing banking, credit unions, MSBs, securities, and futures industries, as well as a state regulatory association. We also interviewed officials from 20 depository institutions, 8 securities firms, and 2 futures firms. For the depository institutions, we interviewed all 5 institutions that had the largest number of suspicious activity report (SAR) filings and randomly selected the remaining 15 based on their number of SAR filings in calendar year 2007. We interviewed the 8 securities firms through the auspices of an industry trade association and interviewed one large and one small futures firm drawn from a list provided by a futures regulator.

We conducted this performance audit in Washington, D.C.; New York, New York; and Chicago, Illinois; from October 2007 to February 2009 in accordance with generally accepted government auditing standards. Those standards require that we plan and perform the audit to obtain sufficient, appropriate evidence to provide a reasonable basis for our findings and conclusions based on our audit objectives. We believe that the evidence obtained provides a reasonable basis for our findings and conclusions based on our audit objectives. Appendix I explains our scope and methodology in greater detail.

RESULTS IN BRIEF

BSA compliance and enforcement efforts are distributed among numerous agencies in accordance with their jurisdictions. Under the BSA regulatory scheme, FinCEN is responsible for the administration of BSA, but delegated its BSA examination authority to the federal banking regulators, SEC, CFTC, and IRS. In addition, the federal banking regulators, SEC, CFTC, securities and futures SROs, and state agencies have independent authority to ensure institutions they supervise comply with all applicable laws and regulations, including BSA/AML-related regulations. FinCEN and most federal regulators have authority to take BSA/AML-related enforcement actions against financial institutions, in some cases directly for violations of BSA and, in others, for violations of rules issued by the regulators. The SROs additionally have rules requiring compliance with BSA. IRS issues letters of noncompliance to institutions and relies on FinCEN for formal civil enforcement action. Justice's role in BSA enforcement is to investigate financial institutions and individuals suspected of criminal money laundering offenses and systemic noncompliance with BSA regulations and prosecute those charged.

While federal agencies have enhanced their BSA/AML compliance programs, opportunities exist to improve interagency and state examination coordination. Notably, the federal bank regulators, in collaboration with FinCEN, have developed uniform examination guidance that each agency uses to examine the institutions under its jurisdiction that have improved collaboration. Similarly, SEC and CFTC, with their respective SROs, have developed examination guidance for the firms they supervise, and IRS and FinCEN have issued an examination manual for MSBs. However, IRS has not fully coordinated MSB examination schedules with the states that license and also examine those businesses, missing opportunities to reduce any potential examination duplication and leverage resources. Further, because federal financial regulators have different institutional approaches to their BSA compliance and enforcement activities, a mechanism to promote greater consistency through compatible activities (particularly when multiple regulators have jurisdiction over the same entity) and to reduce unnecessary regulatory burden is important. However, the agencies do not have such a mechanism and thus may miss opportunities to reduce any unnecessary regulatory burden, a concern identified by industry officials during our interviews, and identify any BSA/AML concerns across industry. Finally, federal banking regulators reported improved transparency and coordination of enforcement actions among federal banking agencies and state agencies, due in part to new interagency enforcement guidance that clarified the circumstances under which regulators could issue a cease and desist order for noncompliance with BSA requirements.

While FinCEN has increased regulatory-dedicated resources, provided examination support through a variety of ways, and made advances in outreach, it could further improve its information-sharing efforts. With its increase in budget authority, FinCEN increased staff dedicated to its regulatory programs, which operate from the Regulatory Policy and Programs Division (RPPD). RPPD provides examination support by commenting on and developing examination guidance and also headed an initiative focused on enhancing risk-based examination approaches. Further, according to FinCEN surveys, RPPD's outreach services were highly rated by industry members surveyed and FinCEN also had undertaken new initiatives, such as establishing a new Office for Outreach Resources. While FinCEN has improved its system for tracking BSA compliance referrals, the lack of a process that facilitates communication between FinCEN and IRS about IRS compliance referrals (combined with IRS's limited enforcement authorities) may delay feedback to IRS- examined entities and allow these institutions to continue operating without correction after deficiencies were identified. FinCEN and IRS have been discussing how to improve the handling of IRS referrals but have not established a mutually agreed-upon process that facilitates communication to ensure timely feedback to institutions. FinCEN also increased the number of information-sharing MOUs with federal and state agencies and surveyed MOU holders. FinCEN and most regulators reported benefits in terms of formalizing data reporting and enforcement coordination procedures. Because FinCEN and CFTC did not finalize their MOU until January 2009, the agencies engaged in limited information sharing while the MOU was being drafted. For example, CFTC officials said that once the MOU was signed, they would consistently track violation data and provide the data to FinCEN along with examination procedures. Without having this mechanism in place to monitor activities, FinCEN and CFTC have not been able to evaluate the results of their efforts to date. FinCEN has taken steps to provide more BSA data analyses to regulators and has been discussing additional products that may be useful for compliance activities. Some securities, futures, and state regulators do not have direct electronic access to BSA data, which impedes examination risk scoping and their ability to independently verify institutions' BSA reporting. FinCEN officials said they finalized a universal data access template in July 2008, and began providing more electronic access to state regulators. However, FinCEN is still working on data access agreements for SROs, and in the meantime, regulators such as SEC's SROs, which conduct the vast majority of broker-dealer examinations, do not have direct electronic BSA data access and must go through FinCEN or SEC to obtain data. The lack of direct access impedes the effectiveness of examination processes by not allowing regulators to assess the extent of BSA activities prior to examinations, and the resulting requests for information strains resources at FinCEN and other regulators.

We are making four recommendations to improve coordination of BSA activities among the federal financial regulators and FinCEN. To better leverage limited examination resources and enhance compliance with a large population of MSBs, we recommend that IRS develop a process for coordinating MSB examination schedules with state agencies. To build on the progress made by FinCEN and federal agencies in coordinating BSA/AML examination processes and to promote consistency in the application of BSA, we recommend that FinCEN and the federal agencies consider developing a mechanism to share and discuss BSA/AML examination procedures and general trends regularly in a nonpublic setting. Further, to improve its efforts to administer BSA, we recommend that FinCEN work with IRS and develop a process that facilitates communication on IRS referrals, and finalize and implement data-access MOUs with several SROs conducting BSA/AML examinations and state agencies that have no direct electronic access to BSA data. IRS agreed with our recommendations and said actions to coordinate examination schedules with state agencies already were underway. In their written responses, all of the agencies agreed with our recommendation that they consider developing a mechanism to conduct regular, nonpublic discussions of BSA examination procedures and trends. In written comments, the FinCEN director concurred with the intent of our recommendations and said he hoped to be situated in the future to meet them.

BACKGROUND

The federal government's framework for preventing, detecting, and prosecuting money laundering has expanded over the course of more than 30 years. With the passage of the Bank Secrecy Act in 1970, for the first time financial institutions were required to maintain records and reports determined to be useful to financial regulators and law enforcement agencies in criminal, tax, and regulatory matters. BSA has three main objectives: create an investigative audit trail through regulatory reporting standards; impose civil and criminal penalties for noncompliance; and improve the detection of criminal, tax, and regulatory violations.

The reporting system first implemented under BSA was insufficient to combat underlying money laundering activity. For example, before 1986, BSA did not contain sanctions for money laundering, although it did contain sanctions for failing to file reports or for doing so untruthfully. To strengthen federal AML initiatives, Congress enacted the Money Laundering Control Act of 1986.[8] In addition to imposing criminal liability for money laundering violations, the act directed each federal banking regulator to require that insured depository institutions establish and maintain a program that would ensure and monitor compliance with the recording-keeping and reporting requirements of BSA.[9]

The Annunzio-Wylie Anti-Money Laundering Act of 1992 amended BSA and authorized Treasury to require financial institutions to report any suspicious transaction relevant to a possible violation of a law or regulation.[10] It authorized Treasury to require financial institutions to carry out AML programs and, together with the Federal Reserve, to promulgate record-keeping rules relating to funds transfer transactions. The act also made the operation of an unlicensed, money-transmitting business illegal under state law a crime.

In 1994, the Secretary of the Treasury delegated overall authority for enforcement of, and compliance with, BSA and its implementing regulations to the Director of FinCEN. FinCEN was established within Treasury in 1990 initially to support law enforcement by providing a government-wide financial intelligence and analysis network, and became a bureau in 2001. Among its current responsibilities, FinCEN issues regulations; collects, analyzes, and maintains BSA-related reports and information filed by financial institutions; makes those reports available to law enforcement and regulators; and tries to ensure financial institution compliance through enforcement actions. According to its strategic plan, FinCEN seeks to ensure the effectiveness of the BSA regulatory framework and facilitate interagency collaboration. FinCEN's RPPD is responsible for BSA regulatory, compliance, and enforcement functions. In August 2004, FinCEN created an Office of Compliance in RPPD to oversee and work with the federal financial regulators on BSA examination and compliance matters.

The most recent expansion of BSA legislation occurred in October 2001 with enactment of the USA PATRIOT Act. Among other things, the act required an entity defined in BSA as a "financial institution" to have an AML program. Each program must incorporate: (1) written AML compliance internal policies, procedures, and internal controls; (2) an independent review; (3) a designated compliance person to coordinate and monitor day-to-day compliance; and (4) training for appropriate personnel. Entities not previously required under BSA to have such a program, such as mutual funds, broker-dealers, MSBs, certain futures brokers, and insurance companies, were required to do so under this act.[11] Moreover, the act mandated that Treasury issue regulations requiring registered securities brokers-dealers to file SARs and provided Treasury with authority to prescribe regulations requiring certain futures firms to submit SARs. Among its other provisions, the act required that Treasury issue regulations setting forth minimum standards for financial institutions regarding verifying the identity of customers who open accounts. The USA PATRIOT Act also required that financial institutions establish due diligence and, in some cases, enhanced due diligence policies designed to detect and report instances of money laundering through private banking and correspondent accounts of non-United States persons; conduct enhanced scrutiny of private banking accounts maintained by or on behalf of foreign political figures or their families; and share information relating to money laundering and terrorism with law enforcement authorities, regulatory authorities, and financial institutions. In addition, nonfinancial institutions also became subject to BSA currency transaction reporting (CTR) requirements where, in the course of trade or business, the business receives more than $10,000 in coins or currency in one transaction (or two or more related transactions).[12]

FinCEN Administers the BSA Framework, under which Many Regulatory Entities Exercise Delegated and Independent Compliance and Enforcement Authorities

The objectives of U.S. financial services regulation are pursued by a complex combination of federal and state government agencies and SROs. Generally, regulators specialize in the oversight of financial institutions in the various financial services sectors, which stem largely from the laws that established these agencies and defined their missions. Under the BSA regulatory scheme, FinCEN is responsible for the overall administration and enforcement of BSA and may take enforcement actions, but federal and state regulators and SROs conduct day-to-day compliance and enforcement activities. Specifically, with respect to examinations for BSA compliance, FinCEN delegated its BSA examination authority to the federal banking regulators, SEC, CFTC, and IRS.[13] The federal banking regulators, SEC, and CFTC also use their independent authorities to examine entities under their supervision for compliance with applicable BSA/AML requirements and regulations.[14] FinCEN has retained enforcement authority and may impose civil penalties for violations.[15] In addition, each of the federal bank regulators also may impose civil money penalties for significant BSA violations, and have specific authority to initiate cease and desist proceedings against the entities they supervise for BSA/AML violations.[16] SEC, CFTC, and their SROs also have authority to enforce their rules requiring BSA/AML compliance; and IRS has very limited enforcement authority delegated by FinCEN.[17] Justice prosecutes criminal violations of BSA, and several federal law enforcement agencies can conduct BSA-related criminal investigations.

FinCEN Administers the BSA and Has Delegated Examination Authority but Retained Enforcement Authority

As noted previously, in 1994, the Secretary of the Treasury delegated overall authority for compliance and enforcement of BSA and its implementing regulations to the Director of FinCEN. Over the years, as more financial activities and types of institutions became involved in the BSA, Treasury delegated BSA examination authority to the federal banking regulators; and to SEC, CFTC, and their SROs. Figure 1 shows the federal agencies and SROs involved in examining for compliance with BSA.

Table 1 summarizes the types and numbers of institutions the federal agencies examine for BSA/AML compliance, and which agency or SRO conducts these examinations.

FinCEN retains BSA enforcement authority and may take enforcement actions independently of, or concurrently with, other regulators. FinCEN's Office of Enforcement conducts independent investigations of BSA violations mostly based on referrals of BSA noncompliance from financial regulators. FinCEN has information-sharing MOUs with the federal banking regulators, SEC, CFTC (as of January 2009), IRS, and some states under which these agencies provide FinCEN information on significant BSA violations and deficiencies found during their examinations. Less frequently, FinCEN conducts investigations based on information from Justice and from its own in-house referrals identified through analysis of BSA data. If a FinCEN investigation results in a decision to take an enforcement action, FinCEN may issue a civil money penalty, depending on the severity of the violation. FinCEN and the financial regulators also try to coordinate enforcement actions. (We discuss coordination of enforcement actions in more detail later in this report.)

Many Federal and State Agencies, as well as SROs, have Independent Compliance and Enforcement Authorities that Encompass BSA/AML Requirements

Independent of Treasury-delegated authorities, the federal banking regulators have general authorities under the federal banking laws to conduct compliance examinations and take enforcement actions against institutions for violations of any applicable law, including BSA. The Federal Deposit Insurance Act specifically provides that the Federal Reserve, FDIC, OCC, and OTS are to prescribe regulations requiring the institutions they supervise to maintain procedures for compliance with BSA requirements and to conduct examinations of those institutions for compliance with reporting and AML provisions of BSA.[18] The Federal Credit Union Act contains the same requirement for NCUA.[19] Federal banking regulators examine whether depository institutions under their supervision are in compliance with BSA/AML requirements concurrently with their examinations for the entities' overall safety and soundness.

Depository institutions can generally determine their regulators by choosing a particular kind of charter—for example, commercial bank, thrift, or credit union—which may be obtained at the state level or the national level.[20] While state regulators charter institutions and participate in oversight of those institutions, all of these institutions have a primary federal regulator if they have federal deposit insurance. The Federal Reserve, FDIC, OTS, and NCUA alternate or conduct joint safety and soundness examinations—including a BSA/AML component—with state regulators, generally using the same examination procedures (shown earlier in table 1). As recently as 2004, about one-third of state banking departments reported not examining for BSA compliance; however, they have taken a more active role in conducting these reviews more recently.[21] FinCEN currently has information-sharing MOUs with 46 state agencies that conduct AML examinations.

As with examinations, the Federal Reserve, FDIC, OCC, and OTS have authority under the Federal Deposit Insurance Act to take enforcement actions against institutions they supervise and related individuals when they determine that an institution or related individual has violated an applicable law or regulation. These agencies also have specific authority to initiate cease-and-desist proceedings for failure to establish and maintain BSA compliance procedures. NCUA also can take enforcement actions under its legislative authorities. Furthermore, state agencies have authority to take enforcement actions against institutions chartered within their state that are in violation of banking legislation.

SEC and CFTC are regulatory agencies with missions that focus on protecting investors, preventing fraud and manipulation, and promoting fair, orderly markets, but the regulatory frameworks for the securities and futures industries are structured differently than those for depository institutions. Consistent with this framework, SEC and CFTC regulate their industries in part through oversight of SROs. SEC and CFTC have authority under the Securities Exchange Act and the Commodity Exchange Act, respectively, to inspect the books and records of firms that they supervise. SEC, CFTC, and their SROs have adopted rules for compliance with BSA/AML requirements.[22]

More specifically, SEC's Office of Compliance Inspections and Examination (OCIE) shares BSA examination responsibilities with securities SROs, which have statutory responsibilities to regulate their own members. The Financial Industry Regulatory Authority (FINRA) provides oversight of the majority of broker-dealers in the securities industry.[23] Other securities self-regulatory organizations include the Chicago Board Options Exchange and Philadelphia Stock Exchange.[24] OCIE and the SROs both conduct BSA/AML examinations for brokerdealers, but only OCIE conducts routine examinations of registered investment advisors and their affiliated mutual funds for BSA compliance as they are not members of an SRO.

CFTC officials said that CFTC does not routinely conduct direct examinations of the firms it supervises; instead, CFTC oversees the examinations conducted by its SROs—the National Futures Association (NFA),which conducts most of the audits, the Chicago Mercantile Exchange, the New York Mercantile Exchange, the Chicago Board of Trade, and the Kansas City Board of Trade. The SROs monitor for compliance with BSA/AML and with their own rules, which include BSA/AML obligations.

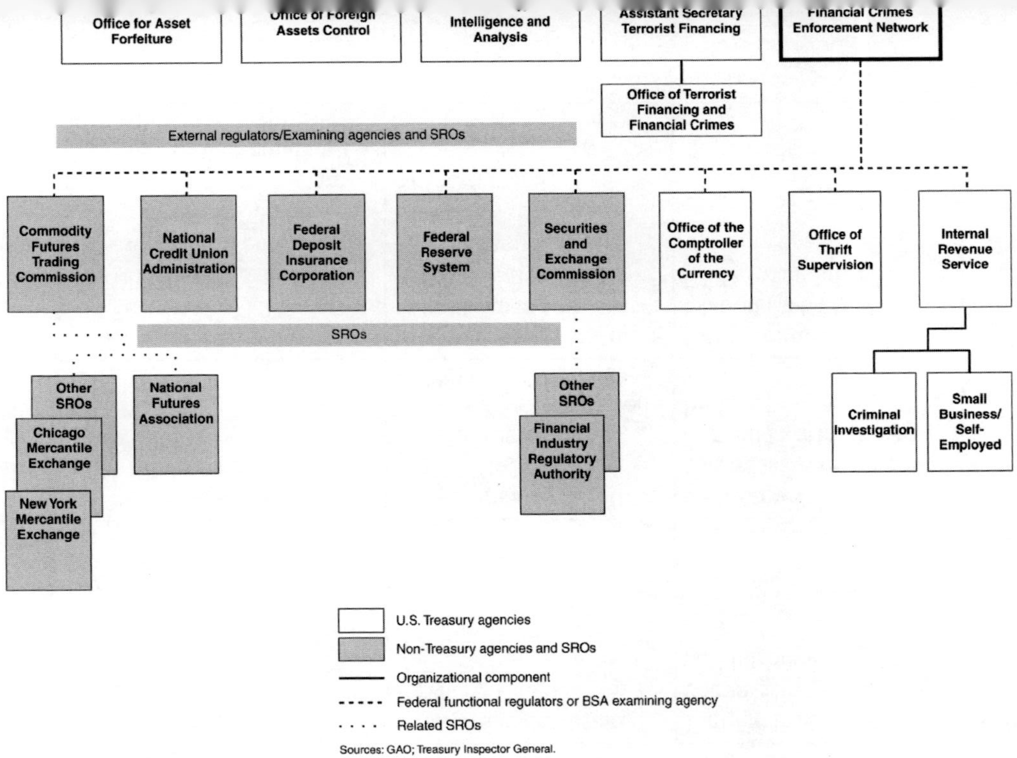

Sources: GAO; Treasury Inspector General.

Note: During the course of our work, in August 2008 the New York Mercantile Exchange merged with the Chicago Mercantile Group, which itself was formed in July 2007 through the merger of the Chicago Mercantile Exchange and the Chicago Board of Trade. We refer to these exchanges separately in this report as each retained its separate DSRO functions.

Figure 1. Overview of Federal Agencies and SROs in the BSA/AML Framework

Table 1. Overview of Federal Agencies with BSA/AML Compliance Responsibilities

	Federal agencies with BSA/AML compliance responsibilities			
	Federal banking regulators (Federal Reserve, FDIC, OCC, OTS, and NCUA)	**SEC**	**C~FTC**	**IRS**
Type of institution under supervision	Insured depository institutions	Broker-dealers, Mutual funds	Futures firms (futures commission merchants and introducing brokers)	MSBs, casinos, and other financial institutions not under the supervision of a federal financial regulator
Number of institutions under supervision for BSA/AML compliance	16,664 depository institutions (as of 9/30/08)	Approximately 5,550 broker-dealers 683 mutual funds (repre-senting 8,752 registered funds) (as of 9/30/08)	154 futures commission merchants and 1,645 introducing brokers	More than 200,000 identified MSBs[a]
Which entity conducts examinations	• FDIC, Federal Reserve, OTS examiners examine supervised entities and may alternate with examiners from state agencies or conduct joint examinations	SEC examiners examine mutual funds and broker- dealers, and SROs examine most broker- dealers (with SEC oversight)	SROs conduct all examinations (with CFTC oversight)	IRS examiners – examinations mainly focus on MSBs and casinos

	Federal banking regulators (Federal Reserve, FDIC, OCC, OTS, and NCUA)	SEC	C~FTC	IRS
	• NCUA examiners examine all federally chartered credit unions. State supervisory authorities conduct BSA examinations at all state-chartered credit unions. NCUA may conduct joint examinations with states, depending on institution risk level. • OCC examiners examine national banks.			

Source: GAO analysis of regulator documentation and data.

[a] In this report we focused on IRS's MSB-related BSA/AML activities, because IRS dedicated the vast majority of its BSA/AML examination resources on MSBs and because other nonbank financial institutions, such as insurance companies and dealers in precious metals and jewels, are new to IRS's examination program. IRS currently has not identified the universe of other nonbank financial institutions, such as dealers of precious metals and jewels.

SEC and CFTC ultimately are responsible for enforcing compliance with their rules and regulations and can institute enforcement actions against firms within their jurisdiction that appear to be in violation of those agencies' BSA-related rules. However, because the SROs overseen by SEC and CFTC have rules requiring compliance with applicable laws and regulations, they typically have front-line responsibility for instituting BSArelated enforcement actions and generally inform SEC and CFTC of such actions. The securities and futures SROs have authority to enforce each of their respective BSA/AML-based rules against their members—generally, broker-dealers and futures firms. They take their own enforcement actions against their members which may include suspending, expelling, fining, or otherwise sanctioning member firms (and their associated persons).

While IRS performs a regulatory function with regard to nonbank financial institutions (NBFI), IRS generally is not considered a "regulator"; it is a bureau within Treasury whose mission is to assist taxpayers in understanding and meeting their tax responsibilities. Unlike the other federal agencies with regulatory functions, IRS does not have independent authority to conduct BSA examinations.[25] Rather, under delegation of examination authority from FinCEN, IRS examines any financial institution not subject to BSA examination by the federal financial regulators.[26] Thus, institutions that IRS examines include MSBs; casinos and card clubs; dealers of precious metals, stones, and jewels; and certain insurance companies. IRS's Small Business/Self-Employed Division, which reports directly to the Deputy Commissioner for Services and Enforcement, conducts BSA compliance examinations of these types of NBFIs. In 2004, IRS created the Office of BSA/Fraud within the division to focus on BSA examinations of NBFIs. As some NBFIs are state-chartered institutions, such as MSBs, IRS also has information-sharing MOUs with many state agencies to facilitate cooperation on examinations.

FinCEN did not delegate to IRS authority to enforce BSA requirements, except for foreign accounts, and IRS does not have independent authority to enforce BSA requirements.[27] IRS can issue a letter of noncompliance and make suggestions for corrective action to institutions it examines for BSA compliance. If significant BSA violations or deficiencies were found or if an institution refused to take corrective action, IRS would refer the case to FinCEN to determine what type, if any, of enforcement action might be appropriate. IRS examiners also may refer cases to their Criminal Investigation unit, if the examiners believe that a willful criminal violation may be involved. IRS Criminal Investigation, IRS's enforcement arm, investigates individuals and businesses suspected of criminal violations of the Internal Revenue Code, money laundering and currency crime, and some BSA requirements. IRS Criminal Investigation investigates BSA criminal violations in conjunction with other tax violations.

Justice Prosecutes Criminal BSA Violations, and Multiple Federal Law Enforcement Agencies can Conduct Criminal Investigations that are BSA-related

While Justice prosecutes criminal violations of the BSA, several federal law enforcement agencies in Justice and the Department of Homeland Security can be involved in the detection and investigation of criminal BSA activity. More specifically, Justice investigates individuals and financial institutions that repeatedly and systemically do not comply with BSA regulations or are involved in criminal money laundering offenses and prosecutes those charged. Referrals to Justice from financial regulators of suspected cases of criminal BSA/AML violations also may trigger a Justice investigation. In addition to prosecutions, Justice has resolved criminal investigations through deferred or nonprosecution agreements and guilty plea agreements, which have included fines, forfeitures, remedial actions, and timelines for implementation.

Within the Department of Homeland Security, the Secret Service, Immigration and Customs Enforcement, and Customs and Border Protection all use BSA data in their investigations. According to Justice officials, most criminal BSA cases against financial institutions start as investigations of individuals involved in illegal activities, such as drug trafficking or money laundering.

While Agencies have Enhanced BSA Compliance Programs, Opportunities Exist to Improve Interagency and State Examination Coordination

Financial regulators have incorporated their BSA/AML responsibilities into their supervisory approaches to compliance and enforcement, but opportunities exist for improved coordination. Federal banking regulators and industry representatives report that their interagency public BSA examination manual increased collaboration on bank examinations. SEC and CFTC have formalized their BSA/AML examination procedures in nonpublic BSA examination modules and coordinate with their SROs on examination issues. IRS developed an MSB examination manual and an overall strategy for NBFI identification and examination with FinCEN, but has not fully coordinated its MSB examination schedules with states, missing opportunities to leverage limited resources. Further, across financial industries, agencies have not established a formal mechanism through which they could discuss compliance processes and trends without industry present. The regulators with enforcement authority issued BSA-related enforcement actions in 2008, and the federal banking regulators improved coordination of their enforcement actions. Officials from the federal banking regulators reported improved transparency and consistency of enforcement actions, due in part to new interagency guidance.

Federal Agencies have Formalized and Cited Improvements to Examination Procedures and Guidance; However, Opportunities Exist for Increased Coordination

In 2005, the federal banking regulators, in collaboration with FinCEN, combined their BSA guidance with examination procedures and made both publicly available in one manual. Since 1986, the federal banking regulators have been required to ensure that institutions under their supervision have AML programs. SEC and CFTC and their SROs use a different approach in regulating their industries—they keep their examination modules nonpublic, but provide public guidance to industry through various methods. With respect to BSA, these agencies and SROs also have coordinated and formalized their examination procedures since the 2001 USA PATRIOT Act required institutions under their supervision to have AML programs. IRS developed an examination manual with FinCEN for MSBs, but does not fully coordinate its examination schedules with state examiners. The financial regulators do not have a nonpublic forum for regularly discussing BSA examination procedures and findings across sectors.

Federal Banking Regulators' Manual and BSA/AML-related Training Have Improved Collaboration and Transparency

Through the development of an interagency BSA/AML examination manual, guidance, and inter- and intra-agency training, the banking regulators have increased collaboration on BSA examinations and the transparency of the examination process. In 2005, the federal banking regulators, in collaboration with FinCEN, published the Federal Financial Institutions Examination Council (FFIEC) BSA/AML Examination Manual, which was updated in 2006 and 2007. The manual provides an overview of BSA compliance program requirements and guidance on identifying and controlling money laundering and other illegal financial activities; presents risk management expectations and sound practices for industry; and identifies examination procedures. All federal and state banking regulators use this manual when conducting BSA/AML examinations, whether they are joint or independent examinations. As mentioned previously, the Federal Reserve, FDIC, and OTS will conduct (on an alternating basis) independent or joint examinations with state agencies. NCUA conducts examinations at all federally chartered credit unions, while state supervisory authorities conduct BSA examinations at all state-chartered credit unions. Depending upon the risks, NCUA may conduct joint examinations with the state authorities at the state-chartered credit unions. OCC supervises nationally chartered banks and federal branches of foreign banks and therefore does not share jurisdiction with state banking regulators. Both federal and state examiners said that the manual helped increase the consistency of examinations among the regulators.

Federal banking regulators also generally share BSA/AML examination workpapers and findings with their state counterparts in cases where they share regulatory jurisdiction over an institution. For example, NCUA officials said that their findings are shared with states to coordinate their reports on joint examinations. State officials we interviewed concurred, stating that they share workpapers in cases where they have federal regulatory counterparts. Several industry officials we interviewed also thought that the federal banking regulators collaborated well with other federal banking regulators on their examinations.

The new examination manual also has improved the consistency and transparency of examinations by providing a framework for examinations, requiring risk assessments and transaction testing, and providing publicly available examination procedures for banks. For example, the manual lists requirements for examination scoping and transaction testing. Officials from one state regulator said the manual has helped answer questions for institutions and regulators, and helped institutions structure their AML programs. All of the federal banking regulators and most of the state banking regulators and banking associations we interviewed consider the process of gathering data for banks and the risk-assessment component of the manual beneficial. As one regulator said, the manual helps an examiner understand an institution's products and services and the steps the institution took to mitigate risks. Most industry officials we interviewed thought the manual provided more consistency to and clearer guidance about the examination process.

While regulators and industry officials said that the manual has been beneficial overall, some banking regulator and industry association officials said that initially it sometimes resulted in longer examinations or additional procedures. Federal Reserve examiners noted that it is important for examiners to apply the risk-based approach, using the minimum procedures where appropriate, and to utilize work previously done by a bank's independent audit, where possible. Similarly, NCUA examiners added that initially the manual resulted in some expanded examinations. However, by using the risk-based approach they are able to focus their resources on the highest areas of risk. Federal Reserve officials added that as examiners have become more familiar with the manual since its adoption, the amount of background reading that examiners need to do in preparing for a BSA/AML examination has decreased. Some officials from the institutions we interviewed were less concerned with the length of the examinations than with some examiners interpreting the manual's requirements too literally or having expectations beyond those expressed in the manual. For example, an official from one large bank said that when the manual was first implemented, regulators were examining "very close to the manual" and interpreted it literally instead of conducting their examinations based on risk. In another case, an official from one small bank that files very few SARs noted that in recent examinations, examiners unnecessarily focused on the bank's record keeping and whether SAR reports were filed on time.

FFIEC serves as the mechanism for the banking regulators to develop interagency BSA/AML guidance for examiners and the industry. FFIEC is also the forum in which banking regulators and FinCEN discuss and draft manual revisions. In addition to its role in developing the manual, the FFIEC BSA/AML Working Group is an interagency group through which the banking regulators develop joint examiner training, such as the AML Workshop and Advanced BSA/AML Specialists Conference. FinCEN officials said that FinCEN specialists also teach at these workshops. Both federal and state banking examiners participate in FFIEC AML workshops and other training sessions offered through their agencies or vendors. In interagency working groups, participants share their knowledge of and experiences with BSA, which federal banking regulator officials have said helped them work toward achieving consistency in their examination processes. Federal banking regulators also train examiners within their own agencies on the new manual.

As a check on their examination programs, including their BSA/AML examination programs, the federal banking regulators conduct quality assurance reviews. The regulators' quality assurance reviews that we examined, which were conducted from 2005 through 2008, indicated that banking examiners were implementing BSA/AML compliance appropriately, with some minor exceptions. For example, reviews from one regulator noted that examiner staff were well trained, devoted significant attention to BSA/AML issues, and generally had well-organized workpapers. Reviews from a second regulator found that examiners complied with BSA/AML guidance, quality control processes were satisfactory, processes for determining enforcement actions and making referrals to FinCEN were sufficient, SAR reviews were timely, and communication between the regulator's headquarters and regions was strong. Another regulator concluded that its examiners demonstrated strong compliance with all issued national and regional guidance for BSA examinations, and found adequate internal controls, no material weaknesses in workpapers, and adequate supervisory and examination resources for evaluating BSA compliance. While reviews generally were positive, they also noted some weaknesses. One regulator recommended that a regional office develop a process for a quality assurance group to periodically review workpapers on a risk-focused basis because of the complexity of the FFIEC BSA/AML examination procedures and also expressed concern about turnover of qualified staff. A second regulator noted a lack of both independent testing and identification of high-risk accounts in one region, and inappropriate recording of a BSA violation in a second region. A third regulator found instances where reported BSA violations were not forwarded to the agency's headquarters.

SEC, CFTC, and Their SROs Coordinated within Their Industries to Formalize Examination Procedures and Also Cited Examination Coordination across Industries

SEC, CFTC, and their SROs share responsibility for oversight of the securities and futures industries, and have worked together to incorporate new BSA/AML requirements into their compliance programs. These agencies take a different approach than the federal banking regulators—they have separate, nonpublic procedures for their examiners and provide public guidance to industry.

In 2006, SEC and what is now FINRA prepared a nonpublic examination module for broker-dealers in an effort to promote consistency in BSA/AML examinations. SEC staff said that the SEC-FINRA module generally formalized procedures and processes that SEC and its SROs already had in place.[28] SEC staff added that their agency has procedures in place for granting access to nonpublic information in response to requests by other regulators. Furthermore, SEC provided all SRO broker-dealer examination modules and procedures to FinCEN for its review and input under their MOU. SEC also has a separate, nonpublic examination module for mutual funds, which it, rather than the SROs, examines.[29] SEC staff explained that BSA/AML examinations of mutual funds are more complex than examinations of broker-dealers because mutual funds do not have their own employees and are managed by investment advisors. Registered investment advisors are rated according to the risk they manage, and those with a higher risk profile are examined more frequently. SEC annually completes approximately 100 mutual fund examinations covering BSA issues.

Working through the Joint Audit Committee, the futures SROs developed a common, nonpublic BSA/AML examination module, which the futures SROs (except NFA) use in their BSA/AML examinations.[30] The Joint Audit Committee updates the BSA module annually and submits the module to CFTC. Unlike SEC, CFTC had not provided the examination modules to FinCEN for its review because the agencies did not have an informationsharing MOU in place until January 2009. (We discuss MOUs in more detail later in this report.) However, CFTC and FinCEN officials informally have discussed procedures the futures SROs use during their BSA/AML examinations.

In lieu of making examination modules public, SEC, CFTC, and their SROs offer public BSA guidance and education through various methods and venues, including the Internet and industry conferences. For example, SEC developed BSA "source tools" for broker-dealers and mutual funds, which compile key laws, rules, and guidance and provide regulatory contact information. The tools are available on SEC's Web site. Securities SROs also provide training and update members on BSA/AML rules and guidance. In addition, FINRA has developed an AML program template for small firms on its Web site that provides possible language for procedures, instructions, and relevant rules and Web sites, among other information. Similarly, CFTC provides information on BSA/AML requirements on its Web site and participates in industry conference panels and outreach efforts with other regulators (in particular foreign regulators). In addition, futures SROs also may provide training, send members updates on new BSA/AML rules and guidance, and participate in industry conference panels to help educate institutions on BSA/AML. For example, NFA provides Web-based training and an AML questionnaire for futures commission merchants and introducing brokers. Overall, industry representatives have been complimentary about the information and education provided by SEC, CFTC, and their SROs; however, they still expressed a desire to have BSA/AML examination modules made public.

SEC, CFTC, and their SROs also have coordinated on multiple-regulator and cross-industry examination issues because many institutions can be registered with more than one SRO or join more than one exchange. For example, broker-dealers can be members of more than one securities SRO. FINRA (which conducts almost 90 percent of broker-dealer examinations) meets with other securities SROs to coordinate examination schedules and ensure that all broker-dealers are covered by examinations. FINRA also has several regulatory agreements to conduct work on behalf of other SROs. In the futures industry, futures commission merchants must be members of NFA and may be clearing members of more than one contract market. Therefore, the Joint Audit Committee assigns an SRO to be the lead regulator, responsible for conducting examinations for each firm with multiple memberships. Examination reports and findings are shared among futures industry SROs where the firm is a member.

Some of the largest SEC-registered broker-dealers also may be registered as futures commission merchants or introducing brokers on futures exchanges. In these instances, FINRA and futures SROs may coordinate informally on BSA/AML examinations of any futures firms that are registered dually as securities broker-dealers. As part of FINRA's information-sharing agreement with NFA, the two SROs meet at least quarterly to share examination results and schedules. Other futures industry SROs obtain FINRA examination results on an as-needed basis. Futures SRO officials said that (1) if FINRA examined an institution's AML program in the last 6 months and reported no major findings and (2) the institution used the same BSA officer and procedures for its securities and futures business, then SRO officials might refrain from conducting the full range of their examination activities. Finally, SEC, CFTC, and the securities and futures SROs participate in Intermarket Surveillance Group meetings.[31]

In addition to working together to help promote consistency in examinations, securities and futures regulators also have programs and procedures—similar to the quality assurance reviews of the federal banking regulators—to review examinations or specific issues. For instance, SEC staff told us that liaisons to each of SEC's regional offices conduct a quarterly review of a representative sample of examinations reports that include AML findings. They added that SEC reviews the examination reports to ensure that AML findings are sufficiently supported and conclusions are valid. SEC staff conducts periodic inspections of FINRA's overall BSA/AML examination program. The purpose of these inspections is to identify any systemic deficiencies or trends in FINRA's BSA/AML program. During previous SEC inspections, SEC and FINRA staff said that SEC identified a few BSA/AML-related deficiencies in specific FINRA examinations. FINRA officials stated that while SEC found isolated weaknesses in some examinations, these findings did not indicate any significant trends. FINRA officials stated they use findings from SEC's reviews to identify areas for additional training. Similar to SEC, CFTC conducts reviews of SROs' examinations, in which CFTC staff review SRO examinations to ensure they are appropriately examining for compliance with futures laws, including BSA. CFTC officials told us that these reviews have not identified any problems with BSA/AML examination programs of the futures SROs.

Although SEC, CFTC, and SRO officials cited coordination on BSA issues, industry officials at large financial companies with whom we spoke had mixed opinions on coordination among the securities and futures regulators. For example, one industry representative said that futures SROs and FINRA coordinated well and shared examination information. The representative also stated that the futures SRO would not conduct its own examination if its review of FINRA's examination workpapers showed the FINRA to be work sufficient. However, another industry representative indicated that they had never seen FINRA and their futures SRO coordinate on BSA/AML examinations.

IRS Has Improved Its BSA Compliance Efforts; However, It Does Not Fully Coordinate Examination Schedules with States

Since our 2006 report, IRS has made improvements in its BSA/AML compliance program by revising guidance, identifying additional NBFIs, and coordinating with FinCEN and the states; however, IRS and state agencies have missed opportunities to better leverage examination resources by not coordinating their examination schedules. In response to a December 2006 GAO recommendation, IRS updated its Internal Revenue Manual to reflect changes in its BSA/AML program policies and procedures and distributed the revisions to IRS staff.[32]

In our 2006 report, we also said that IRS had identified only a portion of the NBFI population. In 2005, IRS's database contained approximately 107,000 potential NBFIs; however, during the same year FinCEN estimated that there could be as many as 200,000 MSBs, the largest group of NBFIs subject to BSA requirements. Through subsequent coordination with FinCEN and state regulators and internal identification efforts, IRS significantly increased the number of identified MSBs. For example, at least three or four times a year, FinCEN sends IRS lists of anywhere from 100 to 300 potentially unregistered MSBs, which FinCEN identified by reviewing SARs from depository institutions that mention unregistered MSBs. Similarly, states that signed an MOU with IRS must provide IRS lists of state-licensed and registered MSBs on a quarterly basis. IRS officials said that the agency found about 20 percent of the new MSB locations as a result of information provided by with the FinCEN and states', but that most of the newly identified MSBs were added due to internal identification efforts. According to IRS officials, in June 2008 the database contained more than 200,000 unique locations of MSBs.

In our 2006 report, we recommended that FinCEN and IRS develop a documented and coordinated strategy that outlined priorities, time frames, and resources needs for better identifying and selecting NBFIs for examination. In response, IRS and FinCEN developed such a strategy.[33] Furthermore, IRS, in concert with FinCEN and state regulators, has developed a BSA/AML examination manual for MSBs that was released in December 2008. The manual contains an overview of AML program requirements, discusses risks and risk-management expectations and sound practices for industry, and details examination procedures. The manual's main goals are to enhance consistency across BSA examiners, promote efficient use of examination resources, and provide guidance to examiners and MSBs about the BSA examination process.

In July and August 2008, IRS and two state regulators tested the feasibility of conducting joint examinations using the new MSB examination manual. Many factors complicate joint examinations—including varying state licensing requirements, coordination of examiner resources, the difficulties of sharing confidential information, and differing examination scope and focus. For instance, one state may require licensing of only money transmitters, while another state also might require check cashiers and currency exchangers to obtain a license. Nonetheless, some state regulators with whom we spoke expressed a desire to conduct joint or alternating examinations with IRS to better leverage state resources. One state regulator said that joint examinations would allow states to issue enforcement actions pursuant to their own state authority against institutions with AML violations since IRS lacks enforcement authority. According to the Money Transmitter Regulators

Association, state financial regulators already conduct joint examinations with other states to leverage examination resources and expertise.[34] IRS officials said they will review and incorporate examiner comments from the joint examination pilot and work with the Conference of State Banking Supervisors to develop formal guidance for IRS and state examiners.

Additionally, IRS has increased the number of its information-sharing MOUs with state financial regulators from 34 in 2005 to 43 as of October 2008. Under the MOU, the state regulators are typically required to provide lists of state-licensed and chartered MSBs, examination reports, information concerning BSA noncompliance, and examination schedules on a quarterly basis to IRS. Also on a quarterly basis, IRS agreed to provide copies of all Letter 1112 (letters of noncompliance sent to institutions with BSA violations), copies of all Letter 1052 (notifications to new institutions of relevant BSA regulations), lists of MSBs in the state, and examination schedules to state financial regulators. According to the MOU, IRS officials and state regulators will meet periodically to review the implementation of the MOU. Following one state financial regulator comment on the usefulness of the information provided in the Letter 1112, IRS officials revised the form letter to include information on the type of institution examined and the activities conducted by that institution.

According to IRS officials, many state agencies are not living up to their responsibilities as stated in the MOU. IRS data show that 28 of 43 state agencies that signed an information-sharing MOU have not provided IRS with MSB information and only 4 of 43 have provided examination schedules. In addition, state financial regulators that send MSB data to IRS do so using different formats, limiting the usefulness of the data for IRS. IRS is working with states to develop a standardized format for all state information, making it easier to provide the information to IRS and for IRS to integrate the information into its database.

While IRS provides MSB information to state regulators, it has not shared its examination schedules with states, contrary to what it agreed to do as part of their MOUs. IRS officials said they provide state regulators with their annual workplans, which include the total number of NBFIs to be examined but not the names of the institutions to be examined. Therefore, the state financial regulators cannot plan their examinations to avoid potential overlap or coordinate joint examinations. One state agency noted that it had conducted examinations of MSBs, only to find out later that IRS had conducted its examinations not long before. Several state agencies said that greater coordination and sharing of examination schedules would help reduce redundancy in examination resources. Best practices in interagency coordination suggest agencies should assess their relative strengths and limitations, identify their mutual needs, and look for opportunities to leverage each others' resources—thus obtaining additional benefits that would not be available if they were to work separately.[35] IRS officials said state regulators would not derive much benefit from IRS providing examination schedules on a quarterly basis because new case files on institutions are sent to field managers often, sometimes weekly, and field managers and examiners have flexibility and discretion to determine their examination schedules. In addition, some institutions on IRS examination lists may not appear on a state regulator's list because of varying state licensing and examination requirements of MSBs. However, by not implementing coordination of examination schedules with states, IRS may have missed opportunities to leverage resources, reduce regulatory duplication, maximize the number of MSBs to be examined, and better ensure BSA compliance with MSBs.

Federal Agencies Do Not Hold Regular, Nonpublic Discussions about BSA Examination Issues, which Could Inhibit Their Ability to Leverage Resources

While all federal agencies have made improvements in their BSA compliance efforts, they have not established a formal mechanism through which they collectively can discuss sensitive BSA examination processes and findings in nonpublic meetings. All federal agencies and some SROs participate in the Bank Secrecy Act Advisory Group (BSAAG)—a publicprivate working group headed by FinCEN that meets twice a year to discuss BSA administration. BSAAG also includes a number of subcommittees on various BSA/AML issues.[36] Representatives from the SROs, industry, and law enforcement agencies are present at these meetings and on some subcommittees. Some regulatory officials have told us that the presence of industry representatives and the number of participants in BSAAG inhibit more detailed discussion on some issues. Further, sensitive information, such as examination processes and findings, cannot be discussed due to the presence of industry.

Some federal agency officials said they have held discussions with regulators of other industries outside of BSAAG, but the discussions generally were held on an informal basis and were not inclusive of all federal agencies. Some banking regulators cited their public manual as a reason for not meeting outside of BSAAG with regulators of other industries. FDIC officials stated, outside of meetings with other federal banking regulators, they had met with several state MSB regulators to understand the MSB examination process and other state roles relating to MSBs. One of the primary goals of these meetings was to determine if they could share information about MSB examinations with some state regulators. SEC staff said they informally have had discussions on BSA/AML issues with federal bank regulators and CFTC. SEC and Federal Reserve staff cited frequent, informal communications between the agencies on BSA issues. Further, SEC and the Federal Reserve signed an MOU in July 2008 under which they can share information on common interests, which could include BSA violations. Under the MOU, if SEC or the Federal Reserve became aware of a significant violation occurring in an institution regulated by the other agency, they would notify the other agency and provide additional information if requested. CFTC officials said that outside of BSAAG, they generally discuss examination procedures only with SEC and FINRA. Similarly, IRS officials stated they have met with regulators on an ad hoc basis when there have been overlapping issues. FINRA officials told us that they had very useful meetings with the Federal Reserve on two occasions (in April and December 2008) during which they discussed BSA examination approaches and findings. These meetings will continue on a biannual basis. In addition, SEC and FINRA staff said that in November 2008, SEC and FINRA staff met with OCC and Federal Reserve staff to share general information about SEC and FINRA's BSA/AML examination programs. While they did not discuss specific examination procedures, FINRA officials said they would be willing to do so if it were useful.

Some industry officials expressed concern about examination overlap and suggested that if regulators collectively could discuss these issues, the collaboration could help decrease resources expended on responding to duplicative information requests and increase the consistency of examination processes. Many of the largest financial institutions are part of a bank or financial holding company structure—companies that could include broker-dealers and futures firms, as well as banks. Therefore, some financial institutions have multiple regulators from various institutions. Industry representatives said that large financial institutions employ enterprise-wide, risk-based AML programs that have many similar elements across business lines. As no single regulator examines BSA/AML procedures for all of the institution's functions, in some cases they must work with several regulators to review the same or similar policies and procedures. In addition, some officials also mentioned that regulators sometimes arrived at different findings when looking at the same BSA processes. For example, one official stated that regulators of different industries reviewed a common AML procedure and arrived at different conclusions—one regulator approved a policy and another requested a wording change.

According to our key practices for collaboration, agencies can enhance coordination of common missions by leveraging resources and establishing compatible procedures.[37] To facilitate collaboration, agencies need to address the compatibility of standards, policies, and procedures—including examination guidance and its implementation. However, because banking-regulator and MSB examination guidance is public and SEC and CFTC guidance is nonpublic, the agencies cannot address these and other sensitive regulatory issues in the existing interagency forum, BSAAG. As a result, the regulators may not be able to gain the benefits of collaboration—leveraging scarce resources and building on the experiences and improvements of other agencies. Furthermore, by not having a mechanism that could provide an overview of examination efforts, regulators may be missing opportunities to (1) discuss BSA/AML concerns from the viewpoint of all financial industries being interconnected and (2) decrease the regulatory burden, where possible, for the institutions under examination by multiple regulators.

Regulators with Enforcement Authority took BSA-Related Enforcement Actions, and Federal Banking Regulators Reported Improved Coordination of Enforcement Actions

The BSA/AML examinations that federal banking regulators, SEC, CFTC, and their SROs conducted resulted in the citation of violations and the taking of informal (in the case of the federal banking regulators) and formal enforcement actions. In our interviews, the federal banking regulators discussed factors potentially influencing BSA compliance in their industry and also reported improved interagency coordination on enforcement actions due, in part, to the issuance of new guidance. SEC and CFTC are kept apprised of enforcement actions that their SROs take through meetings and information-tracking efforts. In contrast, because it does not have the enforcement authority, IRS refers the BSA violations it finds to FinCEN, which takes an enforcement action, if appropriate. Justice pursues cases when it believes BSA noncompliance is criminal.

Table 2. Federal Banking Regulators' BSA/AML Examinations, Most Frequently Cited Violations, and Enforcement Actions, Fiscal Years 2005–2008

	FY 2005	FY 2006	FY 2007	FY 2008
Number of examinations	10,172	10,137	9,601	9,442
Number of violations	8,354	10,970	8,744	6,385
Most frequent violations cited per regulators' regulation				
Independent testing	1,470	2,383	1,263	754
Internal controls	513	1,066	1,177	724
Training	839	1,211	967	788
SARs	351	467	508	643
Compliance program requirements	848	1,144	594	269
Most frequent violations cited to the BSA[a]				
CIP (§103.121)	1,304	999	867	641
CTRs (§103.22)	848	629	720	612
Request for filing reports (§1 03.27)	630	790	788	652
314(a) (§103.100)	370	629	601	469
SARs (§103.18)	134	197	170	98
Number of informal enforcement actions	2,063	6,464	5,067	3,416
Number of formal enforcement actions	74	49	65	37

Source: GAO analysis of banking regulator and FinCEN data.

[a]103.121—Customer identification programs for banks, savings associations, credit unions, and certain non-federally regulated banks; 103.22—Reports of transactions in currency; 103.27—Filing of reports; 103.100—Information sharing between federal law enforcement agencies and financial institutions; 103.18—Reports by banks of suspicious transactions.

Federal Banking Regulators have taken Informal and Formal Enforcement Actions to Promote BSA Compliance among Depository Institutions

The federal banking regulators have taken informal and formal enforcement actions against depository institutions to address BSA/AML concerns. The federal banking regulators can only take enforcement actions under their enabling legislation contained in Title 12 of the United States Code, but these actions can be based on an institution's violation of BSA.[38] Table 2 provides aggregate numbers of examinations, violations, and enforcement actions taken by the federal banking regulators. Under the regulators' AML program rules, in 2008 the most frequently occurring violations concern requirements to independently test an institution's BSA/AML compliance program, train staff on BSA/AML, and maintain internal controls. BSA requires that depository institutions implement and maintain a system of internal controls to ensure an ongoing BSA compliance program. An example of such a control is monitoring for suspicious activity, which one regulator explained can be costly and difficult, and time consuming for an institution to implement. With respect to training, several federal banking regulators said that some banks' staff, even BSA compliance officers, may lack adequate BSA/AML training, especially when such staff are newly hired.

The most frequently cited violations under Treasury's BSA rules are similar across the banking regulators. These violations concern customer identification programs (CIP), CTRs, and requests for filing reports. For example, a violation of CIP requirements could mean that an institution did not implement a written CIP. An institution violating 31 CFR 103.22 did not adhere to the requirement regarding reporting currency transactions in excess of $10,000. Violations of 31 CFR 103.27 could mean that an institution failed to meet the filing and record-keeping requirements for CTRs, reports of international transportation of currency or monetary instruments, or reports of foreign bank and financial accounts. While regulators emphasized that no one factor could explain upward or downward trends in BSA violations, they cited several possible factors influencing these trends—the implementation of the FFIEC BSA/AML examination manual, additional training for examiners and the banking industry, banking regulators more clearly communicating their expectations to institutions, and institutions developing better AML programs. For example, one regulator said that implementing the examination manual may have contributed to a decline in violations by providing guidance to banks on identifying and controlling BSA/AML risk and promoting consistency in the BSA/AML examination process. However, another regulator said that the manual may have led to its increasing number of violations by providing better guidance to examiners. Appendix III provides further information on selected BSA/AML-related enforcement actions taken by all financial regulators.

In response to violations, the federal banking regulators have issued thousands of informal enforcement actions but relatively few formal enforcement actions in recent years. For example, in fiscal year 2008, they issued a total of 3,416 informal and 37 formal enforcement actions. Federal banking regulators said that generally, informal corrective actions will suffice for technical noncompliance or the failure of a portion of the AML program that does not indicate that the entire program has failed. If a compliance violation is significant and remains uncorrected after an informal action has been taken against an institution, a federal banking regulator may then decide to take a formal enforcement action. Banking regulator officials said that formal enforcement actions are public and generally considered more stringent than informal actions because they address more significant or repeated BSA violations. Formal enforcement actions can include cease and desist orders, assessments of civil money penalties (CMP), or supervisory agreements, and are enforceable through an administrative process or other injunctive relief in federal district court.[39] Federal banking regulators said they track enforcement actions through their various management information systems.

Federal Banking Regulators Reported Improved Transparency of Enforcement Actions Due, in Part, to New Guidance

Federal banking regulators reported that new interagency guidance has helped improve the transparency of BSA enforcement. In July 2007, the federal banking regulators issued the "Interagency Statement on Enforcement of Bank Secrecy Act/Anti-Money Laundering Requirements," which clarified the circumstances under which regulators would issue a cease and desist order against a financial institution for noncompliance with BSA requirements. It does not address assessment of CMPs for violations of the BSA or regulators' implementing regulations.

Regulators that we contacted typically stated that the guidance has been beneficial. FDIC officials maintained that with the guidance, bank officials have a better idea of the factors FDIC and other banking regulators take into account before executing a cease-and-desist order. They added that the interagency statement advises that the appropriate regulator may take a different level of action depending on the severity and scope of the bank's noncompliance. NCUA officials said they found that the guidance has led to more consistent enforcement actions taken among the banking regulators in response to cited deficiencies and violations.[40] Both Federal Reserve and OCC officials suggested that the guidance provided more clarity about, or added transparency to, the circumstances under which the agencies will take formal or informal enforcement actions to address concerns relating to a bank's AML program requirements.

Federal banking and state regulators generally coordinate when necessary on BSA enforcement actions.[41] For example, Federal Reserve officials said they usually take (and terminate) actions jointly with state regulators, and a bank must continue to comply with a joint enforcement action until both the Federal Reserve and the state authorities terminate the action. Accordingly, the Federal Reserve and state regulators typically terminate enforcement actions simultaneously. Officials from several state agencies said that as a general rule, they took informal and formal enforcement actions jointly with their federal counterparts, although some state agencies were likely to coordinate only formal actions. Several state officials reported taking few, if any, formal BSA/AML-related actions against depository institutions, especially credit unions.

Several officials from institutions that were examined by multiple federal banking regulators, such as OCC and the Federal Reserve, said that these regulators coordinated well among themselves, while others indicated they were unsure or thought coordination could be improved. Bank officials had mixed views on coordination of enforcement actions between federal and state regulators; some thought the extent of coordination was sufficient, others thought it was lacking, and several simply did not know how extensively these regulators coordinated on enforcement.

Agencies and SROs Take Enforcement Actions in the Securities and Futures Industries

The enforcement actions that SEC, CFTC, and their SROs can use to address BSA compliance can be informal or formal. All SEC enforcement actions are public and formal actions, but the actions of its SROs include informal and formal enforcement processes. SEC staff said that most cited BSA/AML deficiencies are corrected through the examination process. Most examinations conclude with an institution sending SEC a letter stating how it will correct the compliance problem. FINRA officials also said that firms must document the corrective action to be taken to address any issues found during an examination. If SEC examiners find significant deficiencies with a firm's BSA program, SEC staff may refer this to their Division of Enforcement or an SRO for enforcement. In accordance with its MOU, SEC also will notify FinCEN of any significant BSA/AML deficiencies. SEC's Division of Enforcement will assess whether to proceed with an investigation, determine whether a violation has occurred, and if so, whether an enforcement action should be taken against the firm or any individuals. FINRA officials said their enforcement actions are typically fines, the amount of which may vary depending on the egregiousness of the compliance failures, the scope of conduct, and the overall risk of money laundering through the firm.

In fiscal year 2008, SEC and the securities SROs took 25 formal enforcement actions against securities firms (see table 3).

As shown in table 4, in both fiscal years 2007 and 2008, violations in policies and procedures and internal controls and annual independent testing were the most common AML-program-related violations among broker-dealers. With respect to BSA reporting requirements, in fiscal year 2007 the most common violations among broker-dealers were related to CIP requirements and required information sharing. In fiscal year 2008, the most common violations were CIP and SAR requirements. SEC staff said that many of the largest securities firms have had AML programs in place for a while and medium-sized or small firms had AML programs that could be improved.

Table 3. Number of BSA/AML Examinations, Violations, and Enforcement Actions in the Securities Industry, Fiscal Years 2007–2008

	Examinations completed		Violations cited		Formal enforcement actions	
	FY 2007	FY 2008	FY 2007	FY 2008	FY 2007	FY 2008
SEC: broker-dealers	371	336	359	242	0	2
SEC: mutual funds	105	117	12	20	0	0
FINRA (broker-dealers only)	2,195	2,014	3,660	2,984	32	17
Other SROs (broker-dealers only)	259	245	208	119	2	6
Total (broker-dealers/mutual funds)	**2,825/105**	**2,595/117**	**4,227/12**	**3,345/20**	**34/0**	**25/0**

Source: GAO analysis of SEC reports to FinCEN.

Note: This table includes data from fiscal years 2007 and 2008, provided under the FinCEN MOU. Data from previous years cannot be compared as violations were cited differently prior to the MOU, and therefore these data are not included in the report.

Table 4. Number of SEC/SRO Rule Citations and Violations in the Securities Industry under BSA, Fiscal Years 2007–2008

	FY 2007	FY 2008
AML SEC/SRO program rule citations: broker-dealers		
Policies and procedures and internal controls	2,062	1,801
Annual independent testing	753	678
Training	217	129
Policies and procedures for reporting suspicious activity	184	189
Designate individuals for compliance	47	11
Title 31 violations: broker-dealers		
AML program requirements: broker-dealers	3,383	2,864
CIP (§103.122): broker-dealers	606	672
Required information sharing	73	67
SARs (§103.19)	49	83
Nature of records/retention period	44	19
Title 31 violations: mutual funds		
AML program rules for mutual funds	12	18

Source: GAO analysis of SEC reports to FinCEN.

NFA conducts the vast majority of examinations of futures firms and is responsible for all formal enforcement actions taken in recent years (see table 5). The number of BSA/AML-related enforcement actions initiated by NFA decreased from 21 in 2006 to 10 in 2007 and 8 in 2008. Officials added that when new requirements become effective, they usually see an increase in deficiencies related to the new requirements. NFA officials said they reduced the number of deficiencies cited by requiring firms to submit written BSA compliance programs for review during their membership application process. NFA officials said the most common BSA violations cited since 2003 were failure to have annual independent audits and failure to conduct annual BSA training of relevant staff.

Table 5. Number of BSA Examinations, Deficiencies, and Enforcement Actions in the Futures Industry, Calendar Years 2005–2008

	Examinations completed				Exams where BSA deficiencies were found				Formal enforcement actions			
SRO	2005	2006	2007	2008	2005	2006	2007	2008	2005	2006	2007	2008
NFA	303	267	268	183	191	171	159	43	0	21	10	8
Chicago Board of Trade	5	12	6	6	0	1	0	1	0	0	0	0
Chicago Mercantile Exchange	13	5	4	7	0	1	1	0	0	0	0	0
New York Mercantile Exchange	3	4	3	3	2	1	0	0	0	0	0	0
Total	**324**	**288**	**281**	**199**	**193**	**174**	**160**	**44**	**0**	**21**	**10**	**8**

Source: CFTC data.

Note: CFTC provided GAO with year-to-date information for 2008; from January 2008 through August 19, 2008.

CFTC officials said they meet quarterly with SROs to review their open investigations and enforcement actions. If an SRO takes an enforcement action, it will send a copy of the enforcement action to CFTC. CFTC's Division of Enforcement regularly tracked BSA violations investigated and charged by futures SROs, but it did not maintain statistics by the type of violation. Additionally, CFTC receives and reviews examination reports from all SROs, but did not compile BSA/AML examination statistics. In anticipation of finalizing the information-sharing MOU with FinCEN (which the agencies finalized in January 2009), CFTC recently began collecting BSA examination information from the SROs. (We discuss information-sharing MOUs later in this report).

IRS Does Not Have Authority to Take Enforcement Actions and Refers Potential Violations to FinCEN

As previously discussed, IRS does not have its own or delegated authority to issue enforcement actions against NBFIs for BSA violations.44 If IRS finds BSA violations when examining an NBFI, it can send a letter of noncompliance (Letter 1112) and a summary of examination findings and recommendations to the institution, and also include an acceptance statement for the institution to sign. In response to the statement, the institution may agree to implement the recommendations and correct any violations. Generally, IRS would conduct a follow-up examination within 12 months after issuing the letter to determine if the corrective action were taken. In cases where significant BSA violations have been found or past recommendations have been ignored, IRS will refer the case to FinCEN to determine what, if any, enforcement action should be taken. IRS examiners and their managers make the initial determination to refer a case and then an IRS BSA technical analyst reviews the case to decide whether to forward the referral to FinCEN.[45] IRS has referred approximately 50 cases to FinCEN since fiscal year 2006. The referrals include the facts of the case, a summary of the examination, and the violations cited.

During fiscal year 2008, IRS reported citing 23,987 BSA violations and issued a Letter 1112 to 5,768 different institutions (see table 6).

Table 7 provides a summary of the total number of institutions with one of the five violations IRS most often cites.

Table 6. Summary of IRS Quarterly Reports Sent to FinCEN, Fiscal Years 2006–2008

Statistics from quarterly reports to FinCEN	FY 2007 Totals	FY 2008 Totals
Title 31 examinations	8,516	9,238
Number of institutions issued a Letter 1112	5,794	5,768
Title 31 violations cited	33,810	23,987

Source: IRS data and GAO analysis.

Note: IRS signed an information-sharing MOU with FinCEN in April 2005 and did not start providing quarterly reports to FinCEN until the second quarter of 2006. Title 31 examinations are conducted to ensure that institutions are in compliance with BSA requirements.

Justice Pursues Criminal BSA Investigations

Justice officials said they coordinate with financial regulators and FinCEN during criminal BSA investigations and when taking criminal enforcement actions. Most of Justice's BSA cases against financial institutions start as investigations of individuals involved in illegal activities, such as drug trafficking or money laundering. Justice officials also said they have started investigations after receiving referrals from federal regulators.[46] They indicated that having a financial regulator assigned to a Justice investigation can help investigators better understand the financial industry and BSA policies and procedures. Over the last 2 years, both OTS and the Federal Reserve have assigned examiners to Justice investigations. Justice officials work closely with institutions' regulators to obtain and review their examination reports and workpapers, analyze SARs filed, and determine if any civil enforcement actions were taken against the institution. Justice officials said they will coordinate enforcement actions with financial regulators and FinCEN when feasible—checking with both to see if they are planning an enforcement action against the institution. According to Justice, the challenges of coordinating regulatory and criminal enforcement include grand jury secrecy requirements and the differing length and pace of investigations and negotiations. Justice officials said that all their BSA cases against financial institutions have involved systemic, long-term failures in the BSA program and substantial evidence of willful blindness on the part of the institution toward money laundering activity taking place through the institution. In 2005, Justice formalized procedures that require U.S. attorneys to obtain approval from Justice's Asset Forfeiture and Money Laundering Section in cases where financial institutions are alleged to be BSA offenders. Attorneys are to consider factors such as the availability of noncriminal penalties, prior instances of misconduct, remedial actions, cooperation with the government, and collateral consequences of conviction—when determining what type of action, if any, should be taken. Justice officials said they instituted the procedures to provide more review of significant AML cases (in particular, the nature of the violation and its impact) and promote uniformity and consistency in enforcement approaches. According to Justice officials, the new procedures have been well received.

Over the last 3 years, Justice took four criminal BSA enforcement actions against financial institutions (see table 8). All the actions resulted in deferred prosecution agreements (three against depository institutions). The remaining case represents the first criminal BSA enforcement action against an MSB. Justice announced each of the actions on the same day that FinCEN and the regulators announced their civil enforcement actions. The forfeiture amounts generally correspond to the criminal proceeds laundered by the institutions.

Table 7. Number of Institutions with Violations Most Often Cited by IRS, FY 2007–2008

BSA Section	FY 2007 Totals	FY 2008 Totals
AML Program Requirements for MSBs (§103.125)	9,135[a]	12,778[a]
Registration of MSBs (§103.41)	1,823[a]	1,546[a]
Monetary Instrument Purchases (§103.29)	709	713
SARs (§103.20/21)	534	509
CTRs (§103.22/22(b)(2))	422	466

Source: GAO analysis of IRS data.

[a]These figures reflect a combination of several BSA sections.

Table 8. Justice BSA Enforcement Actions, January 2006–October 2008 Year Financial institution

Year	Financial institution	BSA-related violations or investigations	Disposition	Forfeiture amount
2008	Sigue Corporation and Sigue, L.L.C.	Failure to maintain an effective AML program [31 U.S.C. 531 8(h)(1) and 31 U.S.C. 5322(a)]	Deferred prosecution agreement	$15,000,000 forfeiture
2007	American Express Bank International	Failure to maintain an effective AML program [31 U.S.C. 531 8(a)(2) and (h)(1) and 31 U.S.C. 5322]	Deferred prosecution agreement	$55,000,000 forfeiture
2007	Union Bank of California, N.A.	Failure to maintain an effective AML program [31 U.S.C. 531 8(h)(1) and 31 U.S.C. 5322]	Deferred prosecution agreement	$21,600,000 forfeiture
2006	BankAtlantic	Failure to maintain an effective AML program [31 U.S.C. 531 8(h)(1) and 31 U.S.C. 5322(a)]	Deferred prosecution agreement	$10,000,000 forfeiture

Source: GAO analysis of Justice data.

FinCEN Provides Some Effective Outreach and Regulatory Support but could Improve Information-Sharing Efforts

FinCEN has increased resources dedicated to its regulatory programs and provided some effective regulatory support and outreach to industry; however, improvements could be made in its information-sharing efforts with regulators.

From 2001 to 2008, FinCEN staff dedicated to regulatory efforts increased from 36 to 84. FinCEN has coordinated BSA regulation development and supported regulators' examination processes in various ways, including providing input on examination guidance. In 2007, FinCEN created a new unit to provide outreach efforts, such as a helpline, that were well received by industry. FinCEN also has improved its management of referrals from regulators by replacing a paper-based system with an electronic one. However, the lack of an agreed-upon process for communication on IRS referrals may delay timely feedback to IRS-examined entities and allow these institutions to continue operating without correction after deficiencies are identified. Since our April 2006 report, FinCEN has increased the number of information-sharing MOUs with federal and state regulators and has taken steps to assess these MOUs. FinCEN and CFTC recently finalized an MOU, without which they previously did not have an agreed-upon framework for more consistent coordination and information sharing. FinCEN also has been discussing how to improve analytical support with the regulators. However, some state, securities, and futures regulators have limited electronic access to BSA data, which impedes their risk scoping for examinations and ability to independently verify audit information. FinCEN officials said they finalized a regulatory data-access template in July 2008 and have begun providing additional state regulators with direct electronic access, and anticipate providing expanded access to the federal functional regulators.

FinCEN has Increased Regulatory-dedicated Resources, Collaborates with Regulators to Develop Rules and Provides Them with Examination Support, and Provides Well-Received Outreach to Industry

Parallel to its increase in overall budget authority, FinCEN has increased resources dedicated to its regulatory programs. FinCEN officials said they consult with other regulators and examining agencies as necessary when developing rules and implementing regulations, provides examination support to regulators, and conducts BSA-related training sessions and events for industry and regulators.

Table 9. FinCEN Budget Authority, Civilian Full-time Equivalent Employees, and Regulatory-Dedicated Staff, Fiscal Years 2001–2007

	FY 2001	FY 2002	FY 2003	FY 2004	FY 2005	FY 2006	FY 2007
FinCEN budget authority (in millions of dollars)	$38	$48	$52	$58	$72	$73	$73
FinCEN civilian full-time equivalent (direct)	174	200	229	249	267	296	302
Regulatory-dedicated staff	36	51	55	59	75	76	77

Source: U.S. Budget Appendix and GAO analysis of FinCEN data.

FinCEN Has Increased Resources Dedicated to Its Regulatory Programs

As shown in table 9, FinCEN's budget authority and regulatory-dedicated staff have grown from fiscal year 2001 through fiscal year 2007. FinCEN budget authority grew from $38 million in fiscal year 2001 to $73 million in fiscal year 2007. Since 2005, the bureau's budget authority essentially has been flat. From fiscal year 2001 through fiscal year 2007, the number of FinCEN staff dedicated to regulatory policy and programs approximately doubled, from 36 to 77. The total number of FinCEN staff increased nearly 75 percent from 174 to 302.

FinCEN regulatory policy and program staff work in RPPD, which consists of the Offices of Regulatory Policy, Compliance, Enforcement, Regulatory Analysis, and Outreach Resources. According to FinCEN officials, these staff work on issues that involve multiple financial sectors, although many employees have subject matter expertise for particular industries or sectors. As of September 2008, FinCEN officials said that RPPD had a staff of 84. Since 2001, several regulators also have provided detailees to FinCEN to supplement expertise in particular areas or work on specific projects. For example, from 2007 through 2008, a detailee from the Federal Reserve worked on an industry survey about the potential effects of rule making related to FinCEN's cross-border wire transfer study and served as a subject matter expert regarding payment systems.[47] And from 2002 through 2005, two IRS detailees to FinCEN worked with RPPD to resolve multiple outstanding compliance issues. In addition, in 2005-2008, FDIC officials said that the agency provided 11 detailees to assist with report processing and other assignments.

FinCEN and Regulators Collaborate on Implementing BSA Regulations

BSA provides Treasury with overall regulatory authority to administer the act and authorizes Treasury to issue regulations, sometimes jointly with federal financial regulators, to implement BSA requirements.[48] FinCEN, the bureau within Treasury responsible for administering BSA, has overall responsibility for Treasury's BSA regulatory program. Within FinCEN's RPPD, FinCEN officials said that the Office of Regulatory Policy is responsible for developing, modifying, interpreting regulations and consults as necessary with other regulators and examining agencies.

Depending upon the subject matter of a regulatory initiative, FinCEN officials said their interactions with regulators on BSA implementing regulations can range from extensive collaboration to a notification that regulations are available. In addition to meetings with regulators, FinCEN officials stated they obtain feedback from regulators on BSA issues through BSAAG and its multiple subcommittees. Referring to the USA PATRIOT Act, some federal agency officials observed that the development of some regulations was collaborative and an improvement compared with other processes in which the regulators were less involved.

FinCEN officials said their work in recent years with SEC and CFTC—an outgrowth of the USA PATRIOT Act—generally has been collaborative, particularly given the newness of the securities and futures industries to the BSA/AML regulatory framework. SEC staff said they often met with FinCEN to discuss BSA issues (including rules development and related FinCEN guidance). Also, FinCEN sometimes participated in SEC's quarterly BSA meetings with the SROs, discussing the scope of reforms and clarifying guidance or other issues. FINRA officials said that FinCEN and SEC directly collaborated on rules for broker-dealers, and FINRA was able to provide input in these discussions only through SEC. While FINRA officials said that they coordinated well with SEC, they felt that direct and earlier coordination with FinCEN on rule and guidance development would have increased the efficiency of the process.

CFTC officials stated that work with FinCEN on drafting of futures-related BSA/AML rules and guidance has been collaborative. For instance, as required by BSA, FinCEN and CFTC jointly issued regulations in 2003 for futures commission merchants and introducing brokers requiring them to establish CIPs.[49] However, according to CFTC officials, the rule resulted in some confusion about its applicability in situations where more than one futures commission merchant was involved in a transaction with the same customer.[50] In April 2007, FinCEN and CFTC jointly issued guidance to clarify the responsibilities in such a transaction.[51] NFA officials said the guidance has been well received by its members and clarified issues surrounding a firm's BSA/AML role with its customers.

FinCEN and IRS officials had differing views on the degree of collaboration that occurred during the revision of MSB-related regulations. As discussed previously, FinCEN and IRS completed a coordinated strategy in 2008 to better identify and select NBFIs for examination. The coordinated strategy states that FinCEN would work with regulatory partners to explore the feasibility of removing or exempting from the definition of MSBs certain types of transactions or subcategories of MSBs that pose relatively little risk of facilitating financial crimes. At the time of this report, FinCEN was in the process of incorporating revised MSB definitions into its guidance and regulations. Although legislation does not require FinCEN to conduct joint rule making on MSB issues, FinCEN officials stated that RPPD staff have briefed other offices and divisions in FinCEN as well as IRS, federal banking regulators, Treasury officials, various law enforcement agencies, and the BSAAG NBFI subcommittee on the proposed MSB rule making. The BSAAG NBFI subcommittee, of which IRS is a member, also sent a list of issues for FinCEN to consider when redefining MSBs, which FinCEN officials said they reviewed. FinCEN officials said they met with IRS staff in May 2008 to discuss the advanced notice of proposed rule making.

According to FinCEN officials, they also developed a majority of their guidance and administrative rulings by reviewing questions received from the financial industry through their Regulatory Helpline (which institutions and regulators may call with questions) or other correspondence. For example, FinCEN officials said they review questions asked of the Office of Outreach Resources to determine what issues concern industry, and the results of the reviews are forwarded to the Office of Regulatory Policy. (We discuss the Office of Outreach and FinCEN helplines in more detail below.)

FinCEN Supports Regulators' Examination Activities by Providing Input on Guidance and Addressing Specific Issues

FinCEN and RPPD's Office of Compliance provide examination support for financial regulators in various ways. These methods include providing input on examination guidance and working with regulators to address specific issues (such as risk scoping). For instance, FinCEN actively participates in FFIEC working groups to revise the FFIEC BSA/AML manual and develop examiner training.[52] In February 2007, FinCEN established a working group comprising federal and state agencies, with the goal of identifying and implementing several large initiatives to more effectively regulate and supervise the activities of MSBs. As previously discussed, FinCEN, IRS, and state regulators worked together in this forum to develop an MSB BSA/AML examination manual that was issued in December 2008. FinCEN officials said they will work with IRS and the manual working committee to develop a roll-out plan and provide training to IRS and state examiners, and the working group will continue to meet to address other MSB-related issues.

FinCEN also has reviewed SEC's and its SROs' nonpublic examination procedures. Additionally, SEC and FinCEN cooperated to develop Webbased tools ("AML source tools") that compile applicable BSA/AML rules and regulations for mutual funds and broker-dealers as well as other helpful information and contacts. SEC staff stated that they also developed "plain English" guidance on the examination process to be made public in response to further industry requests for access to SEC's nonpublic examination module. SEC provided the draft guidance to FinCEN for its input; however, FinCEN officials said their review is on hold because their staff are working on other priorities and industry already has the AML source tools as guidance. While FinCEN has worked similarly with CFTC on guidance to its industry, FinCEN officials said that CFTC's SROs have not provided their examination module and procedures to FinCEN but intended to do so after the information-sharing MOU between FinCEN and CFTC was finalized. However, FinCEN and CFTC officials stated they have held meetings on the examination procedures of futures SROs.

As part of the effectiveness and efficiency initiative announced by the Treasury Secretary in June 2007, FinCEN has been studying how the regulatory agencies are approaching risk scoping for examinations. Its goal is to develop new tools and guidance that would enable agencies to better direct their examination resources. FinCEN officials stated they evaluated tools and processes that allow examiners to analyze information and patterns in BSA data from a specific institution to help identify areas that may require closer review, and jointly identified ways to enhance these tools. For example, FinCEN officials said they and the federal banking regulators are developing an enhanced BSA data analysis tool to incorporate into pre-examination scoping processes that will allow the federal banking regulators to better target their resources. Federal banking regulator officials stated that the tool would help them better analyze BSA data information for a particular institution, but not to conduct analyses across institutions.

In addition to supporting regulators' examination efforts and undertaking-process-or issue-specific initiatives, FinCEN officials said it also has produced targeted financial institution analyses. These are produced after a regulator makes a specific request for detailed analytic information related to a particular institution or individual. Office of Regulatory Analysis staff said they have collaborated with regulators to produce 42 such reports during fiscal year 2007 and through the first three quarters of fiscal year 2008.

With respect to its role in term's of achieving greater BSA/AML examination consistency, FinCEN officials stated that, resources permitting, they would like to increase their efforts in areas such as examiner training, developing and providing additional compliance referrals to regulators, periodically joining examiners in the field, and conducting additional macro-level analysis of BSA compliance. (We discuss FinCEN's analytical products in a later section.) FinCEN officials said they have held various meeting with regulators to discuss their examination processes, but that they have not held meetings inclusive of all regulators. Further, as discussed previously, without an informationsharing MOU in place, FinCEN had been unable to obtain examination procedures for the futures industry—hindering its ability to review issues of BSA/AML examination consistency.

Offices within FinCEN Coordinated to Provide Outreach that was Well received by Industry

FinCEN has implemented new outreach initiatives and conducted support efforts on BSA guidance that were well received by industry. The Office of Outreach Resources was created in 2007 and has primary responsibility for operating the Regulatory Helpline that industry and regulators may call with BSA-related questions. FinCEN staff also operate the Financial Institutions Hotline, which financial institutions may call to report suspicious activity related to terrorist financing. For the past 3 years, FinCEN has surveyed customers who use the Regulatory Resource Center—which includes the Helpline and FinCEN's Web site. According to FinCEN's surveys, in all 3 years, FinCEN staff calculated more than 90 percent of respondents—primarily industry representatives—favorably rated the guidance they received.[53]

FinCEN officials said that as part of its efforts to make the administration of BSA more efficient and effective, FinCEN published proposed rules in the Federal Register in November 2008 that centralize, without substantive change, BSA and USA PATRIOT Act regulations to a new chapter within the Code of Federal Regulations. FinCEN officials said that the proposed rules would streamline BSA regulation into general and industry-specific parts, with the goal of enabling financial institutions to more easily identify their BSA responsibilities.

The Office of Outreach Resources also coordinates with BSAAG and supports speaking engagements to the financial industry and regulatory groups. FinCEN officials told us they have facilitated BSAAG subcommittee meetings (such as ones on banking, insurance, law enforcement, SARs, and securities and futures) throughout the year. In 2007, FinCEN reported participating in almost 100 domestic and overseas outreach events on BSA issues relating to banking, securities, futures, MSBs, jewelers, casinos, insurance companies, and credit unions. Industry officials with whom we spoke generally were positive about FinCEN's outreach to industry, including these events and some of the public products available on FinCEN's Web site. Banking industry association officials felt that FinCEN had been helpful in listening to concerns of the banking industry. Securities industry officials stated they thought FinCEN had been very responsive to inquiries from broker-dealers and found some of FinCEN's publicly available reports to be very useful, including "SAR Activity Review: Trends, Tips, and Issues" and mortgage fraud reports. FinCEN officials presented these reports at events and included a discussion of how SARs have contributed to law enforcement investigations. A representative of a futures firm with whom we spoke said the firm used the SARs publications as part of its training program. Securities SRO officials said they felt FinCEN was doing an excellent job of industry outreach, in particular showing the industry how BSA data filings were used effectively to prosecute money laundering and other financial crimes.

In January 2008, FinCEN's Office of the Director—with participation from RPPD, the Analysis and Liaison Division, the Technology Solutions and Services Division, and the Office of Chief Counsel—began a new outreach program to the financial community. By developing a better understanding of the needs and operations of institutions, FinCEN officials suggested that the agency will be in a better position to help institutions effectively operate BSA/AML programs. The outreach program's goals include learning how institutions' BSA/AML programs and analytical units operate. The first stage of the outreach program is targeted to the 15 largest depository institutions. According to FinCEN, they will expand outreach to other depository institutions and industry sectors, but have not finalized the timetable for the later stages of the program.[54]

FinCEN has Improved Tracking for Incoming Compliance Referrals; However, Lack of a Process for IRS Referrals could Impede BSA Compliance Activities

In 2006, FinCEN implemented an automated Case Management System (CMS) to track its processing of BSA compliance referrals, which replaces a paper-based system. While its efforts to track referrals have improved, FinCEN processing times for IRS referrals, combined with IRS's limited enforcement authority, may have limited IRS's BSA compliance activities among NBFIs.

FinCEN Has Improved Its Compliance Referral Tracking System

According to their MOUs with FinCEN, the federal banking regulators, SEC, and IRS are to inform FinCEN of any significant potential BSA violations and provide BSA-relevant examination reports. In 2006, FinCEN implemented an automated system—CMS—to track these BSA compliance referrals.[55] Prior to CMS, FinCEN tracked BSA compliance referrals manually through a paper-based system. FinCEN officials stated that CMS enables RPPD's Offices of Compliance and Enforcement to track cases from receipt to final disposition, analyze the data, and produce management reports.[56] Figure 2 depicts the overall process by which FinCEN receives and tracks these referrals.

As shown in figure 2, the Office of Compliance receives referrals from regulators or referrals that are self-reported by institutions and, after receipt, opens corresponding cases in CMS.[57] These matters are assessed by compliance specialists who, in making their assessment of each referral, consider factors such as

- whether the violation was systemic or technical;
- whether the violation was willful or a result of negligence;
- how long the deficiency existed; and
- whether the violation surfaced through self-discovery or an examination.

Compliance staff must complete the initial assessment within 60 days, after which the case is reviewed by a compliance project officer, the compliance program manager, and, finally, the assistant director of compliance. As part of these assessments, Office of Compliance staff may request additional data analysis from the Office of Regulatory Analysis or additional documentation from the institution's regulator. Federal banking regulator and SEC staff confirmed that FinCEN staff have requested additional information about their referrals.

After a referral is assessed, Office of Compliance management decide whether to take one of the following actions: (1) close a case with no action; (2) send a notification letter to the institution indicating that the regulator informed FinCEN of the matter, and nothing precludes FinCEN from further action if FinCEN or the regulator finds that all corrective actions have not been implemented; or (3) present the matter to FinCEN 's Regulatory Enforcement Committee. FinCEN officials estimated that its Office of Compliance has forwarded approximately 6 percent of referrals to its Office of Enforcement. The Regulatory Enforcement Committee consists of compliance and enforcement staff who review the case and decide whether to forward it to the Office of Enforcement for further investigation After it is decided that a case is to be referred to the Office of Enforcement, the case is closed by Office of Compliance staff in CMS and the Office of Enforcement opens a new Enforcement case in CMS.

FinCEN officials said that the fundamentals of the enforcement investigative process are the same, regardless of the source of the referrals. And, as with Compliance staff, Enforcement staff may request additional data analysis or documentation when making their decisions. They document their investigation in a recommendation memorandum to the Assistant Director of the Office of Enforcement. After the assistant director has reviewed the case, Enforcement staff contact the referring agency to discuss the matter. If no action is warranted, Enforcement closes the case. If a CMP is warranted, Enforcement issues a charging letter to the financial institution. The financial institution is required to respond in writing within a specified period (usually 30 days from the date of the letter). The assistant director and an enforcement specialist then review the financial institution's written response to determine whether to proceed with a CMP negotiation meeting or close the matter with an alternative action, such as a warning letter, or no action. FinCEN Enforcement officials said that if a warning letter is issued, it will be routed internally for approval through the Associate Director of RPPD and a copy will be sent to the relevant regulator. FinCEN's Director iterated in an October 2008 speech that FinCEN considers enforcement actions only when a financial institution exhibits a systemic breakdown in BSA compliance that results in significant violations of its BSA obligations. Table 10 shows the number of referrals RPPD received during fiscal years 2006 though 2008, the number of cases closed within the Office of Compliance and Enforcement, and average processing times.

FinCEN officials told us that they have striven to take joint or concurrent enforcement actions with other federal and state agencies. In very rare cases, the Office of Enforcement may initiate a case directly—that is, without a referral. Since our last report in April 2006, FinCEN has taken one independent action against a depository institution under BSA. The Office of Enforcement may develop a case based on information from Justice or receive internal referrals developed from internal review and analysis of BSA data. For instance, FinCEN officials cited a case in which their analysis uncovered that an institution had been leaving a description field in their SAR filings blank. This was not a technical error, but a significant deficiency resulting in a CMP being assessed against the institution.

In addition to receiving and processing referrals from regulators, FinCEN may uncover and refer compliance matters of a more technical, rather than systemic or significant, nature to the regulators. FinCEN stated that RPPD's Office of Compliance dedicates substantial resources to reviewing SAR filings for data quality issues and refers potential BSA deficiencies or violations to regulators. In its 2007 annual report, FinCEN noted that it referred 83 matters concerning potential BSA deficiencies or violations to regulators with which it has MOUs. Officials from most federal banking regulators confirmed that FinCEN provided them with referrals about institutions under their supervision that were filing incomplete or technically inaccurate SARs. FDIC officials cited instances in which such information led to identifying software problems that had been negatively affecting many institutions. FDIC officials also said that FinCEN once provided them with information regarding a possible money laundering scenario. Other federal banking regulators stated that the referrals they received from FinCEN were of a technical nature and did not prompt an examination.

Lack of Agreed-upon Process that Facilitates Communication about Processing IRS Referrals could Delay Timely Feedback to NBFIs

According to IRS officials, long delays in processing referrals and a lack of an agreement on time frames have limited IRS's BSA compliance activities among NBFIs. Unlike the federal financial regulators that have independent enforcement authority to issue informal and formal enforcement actions, IRS officials can send only a Letter 1112 to an institution, which includes a statement that a copy of their report is required to be sent to FinCEN and that

FinCEN will determine if penalties under BSA are to be imposed (see discussion in previous section).[58] Therefore, when IRS finds an NBFI with significant BSA deficiencies, it must refer the case to FinCEN for further action.[59] In fiscal years 2006—2008, IRS sent approximately 50 referrals to FinCEN. After a referral is made to FinCEN, IRS officials said they do not conduct a follow-up visit with the institution to determine if corrective action has been taken until FinCEN makes a determination on the referral, as they do not want to take any actions that might negatively affect a potential FinCEN enforcement action.

IRS officials believe FinCEN's response time is too long. FinCEN officials stated that IRS referrals often require follow up for additional information or supporting documentation which affects processing times. As noted in table 10 above, FinCEN's average processing time for all referrals in fiscal year 2008 was 208 days in its Office of Compliance and an additional 277 days if a case was referred to its Office of Enforcement. IRS and FinCEN officials met in early 2008 to discuss processing times and what information an IRS referral should contain. IRS officials said they have seen progress in the last several months, with more IRS referrals being processed. Although IRS officials stated that they would like an agreement with FinCEN on referral processing times, no formal agreement has been negotiated. FinCEN officials said that they do not have established time frames for responding to referrals because response time often varies depending on the thoroughness of the referral and the need for follow up with the examiner. They said that processing of referrals also depends on interagency coordination. For example, law enforcement authorities might ask FinCEN to refrain from advancing certain cases because of pending criminal investigations. While FinCEN and IRS recently have been meeting more frequently to discuss IRS referrals, no formal agreed-upon process exists to address IRS referral issues and provide more timely feedback to IRS-examined institutions on their AML efforts. The lack of an agreed-upon process for handling referrals, combined with IRS's inability to take certain enforcement actions on its own, may result in these institutions continuing to operate without correction, potentially remaining out of compliance with BSA.

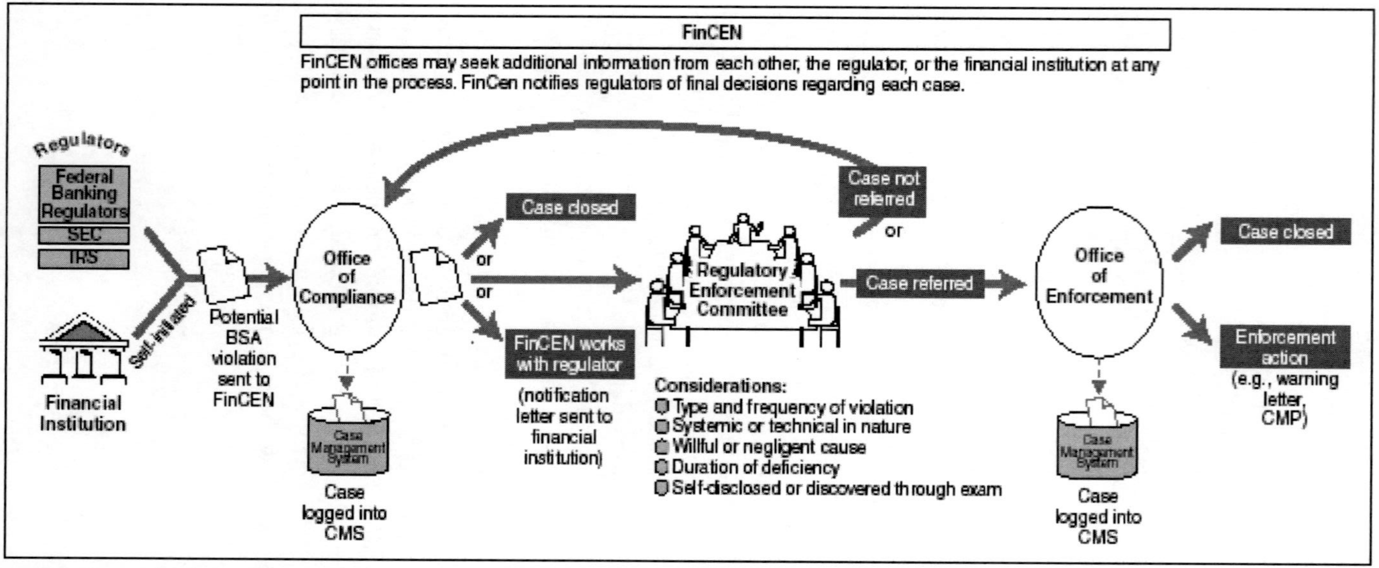

Sources: GAO analysis of FinCEN documentation; Art Explosion (images).

Figure 2. FinCEN's Tracking Process for BSA Compliance Referrals

Table 10. Number of Cases Processed in FinCEN's Offices of Compliance and Enforcement and Average Processing Times, Fiscal Years 2006–2008

		Compliance		Enforcement[a]	
Fiscal year	Total referrals received (source: regulatory agency/ self-reported)[b]	Number of cases closed	Average processing time (days)	Number of cases closed	Average processing time (days)
2006	268 (242/26)	241	198	13	349[d]
2007	241 (220/21)	248	275	18	433[d]
2008	275 (225/50)	265	208[c]	17	277

Source: FinCEN data from CMS.

[a]These figures were adjusted to reflect the number of days that cases were processed minus the number of days cases were on hold pending a law enforcement investigation.

[b]The number of cases processed in the Offices of Compliance and Enforcement may not add up to the total number of referrals received each fiscal year, as not all referrals may have been processed in that year and would have carried over to the follow year.

[c]This figure is adjusted to reflect the number of days that a compliance case was processed minus the days cases were on hold or placed on monitor status. This figure is manually calculated and subtracted from the "raw" number—235 days—for fiscal year 2008. In 2008, FinCEN began excluding days from the average processing time when the referrals process was on "hold" (for example, waiting for information from a regulator).

[d]These figures include cases that were in the Office of Enforcement inventory prior to the creation of the Office of Compliance. The longer processing times for these years reflect the fact that additional time was spent by enforcement specialists to start some cases and obtain data and information—a process now conducted by the Office of Compliance.

MOUs have Improved Coordination with Federal Banking Regulators and SEC; and FinCEN and CFTC recently signed an MOU

FinCEN officials have increased the number of information-sharing MOUs with regulatory agencies, which has improved coordination of enforcement actions and BSA data reporting for the banking and securities industries. FinCEN officials said that through the information-sharing MOUs they made progress in developing their relationships with the federal banking regulators, SEC, and IRS. Since our April 2006 report, FinCEN had implemented an MOU with SEC (in December 2006), and as of October 2008, established MOUs with 46 state agencies. After several years of drafting, FinCEN and CFTC finalized information-sharing and data-access MOUs in January 2009.

Federal Banking Regulators and FinCEN Reported that MOUs Resulted in Improved Processes for and Coordination of BSA Reporting and Enforcement

FinCEN officials said that the MOU process significantly increased the level of information sharing with the federal banking regulators since its implementation in 2004. FinCEN officials also said that the federal bankin g regulators made good faith efforts to comply with the MOU and provide d FinCEN with reports on time. Official s from most federal banking regulators stated that their 2004 MOU significantly strengthened interaction with FinCEN and provided structure for coordination on enforcement actions and information sharing. In addition, FinCEN's Director together with Treasury's Under Secretary for Terrorism and Financial Intelligence meets quarterly with the principals of the five federal banking regulators to discuss coordination and BSA admini stration for the industry.

While federal banking regulator officials emphasized that they may take enforcement actions independent of FinCEN under their own authorities, they ensure that FinCEN is aware of these actions as agreed upon in the MOU with FinCEN. Federal Reserve officials said that such information sharing generally involves referral of all BSA/AML-related examination issues that are resolved through informal and formal enforcement actions. They explained that when taking an informal action—such as a commitment letter or MOU—they provide notice to FinCEN. OTS officials said they have quarterly meetings with FinCEN during which they discuss any BSA-related informal or formal actions, as well as any related matters. Moreover, federal banking regulators said they make FinCEN aware of formal actions, such as CMPs or written agreements, well in advance of when the actions will be taken. For example, if the regulators are going to impose a CMP, they will inform FinCEN early enough to ensure the process is fully coordinated. Federal Reserve officials said that since the 2004 MOU, they imposed all BSA/AML-related CMPs concurrently with FinCEN penalties.[60] NCUA officials also said they make FinCEN aware of informal and formal actions, and would coordinate with FinCEN prior to the issuance of a CMP, if necessary. OCC officials said they also coordinate any CMPs with FinCEN and that in recent years FinCEN has been much quicker in assessing CMPs in conjunction with OCC. They cited a case prior to the implementation of the MOU—the Riggs Bank case—during which they said they had to wait more than a year to issue a CMP in coordination with FinCEN.[61] FDIC and OTS also noted they have worked closely with FinCEN in the past few years on the development of BSA/AML-related enforcement actions against several institutions.[62] (App. III contains examples of BSA/AML-related enforcement actions.)

Several federal banking regulators also cited their 2004 MOU with FinCEN as beneficial in terms of improving agencies' internal processes for tracking violations and enforcement actions. Some federal banking regulator officials said that as part of responding to the information- sharing requirement of the MOU (that is, providing FinCEN with quarterly BSA examination, violation, and enforcement data), they established centralized, automated data collection programs that have improved the quality of their BSA examination data. For instance, FDIC officials said their agency internally standardized the processes for collecting BSA data as a result of the MOU. Federal Reserve officials also reported that enhancements to the agency's data management system have streamlined the information it gathers for FinCEN under the MOU.

While federal banking regulators have made improvements in their systems for collecting and reporting BSA/AML-related data, differences remain in how they cite violations. In our 2006 report, we found that the federal banking regulators were using different terminology to classify BSA noncompliance and recommended that FinCEN and the federal banking regulators discuss the feasibility of developing a uniform classification system.[63] Since our report, FinCEN and the federal banking regulators established an interagency working group that is reviewing guidance relating to the citing of BSA violations and is considering additional guidance on citing systemic versus technical AML violations. One federal banking regulator stated that while BSA/AML violation is generally comparable, federal banking regulators have different definitions for the same terms. However, to implement their MOU, FinCEN official s said that they discussed what a "significant violation" means and tha t they came to agreement (see previous discussion).

FinCEN's MOU with SEC Has Improved Information Sharing

SEC and FinCEN staff stated that their December 2006 MOU had been beneficial overall, although it is still in the relatively early stages of implementation. Pursuant to their MOU, SEC shares examination findings with FinCEN after a significant BSA deficiency is found. For enforcement actions, SEC provides notice to FinCEN prior to the action becoming public.

In addition, SEC receives information from the SROs about BSA/AML-related significant deficiencies or potential enforcement a ctions and provides that information to FinCEN. SEC and FinCEN staff said the MOU is still in the early stages of implementation and SEC and FinCEN recently met and reached agreement on steps to further coordination.

SEC staff also said that its agency's MOU with FinCEN has provided a framework for the quarterly collection and reporting of BSA/AML examination, violation, and enforcement action data. While SEC staff stated they had provided FinCEN with data prior to the MOU, it was on a more limited basis. Prior to the MOU, SEC cited BSA violations under provisions of the USA PATRIOT Act. Under the MOU, SEC cites BSA, which allows for more specific citations. As a result, under the MO U, SEC provides additional examination information regarding BSA violation categories and subcategories. For example, SEC previously would cite a violation relating to CIPs under Section 326 of the USA PATRIOT Act. Because of the MOU, SEC can determine which of the multiple subcategories of BSA it may cite for deficiencies in a firm's CIP. (See table 3 earlier for these data.)

FinCEN and CFTC Recently Signed an MOU, without Which the Agencies Engaged in Limited Information Sharing

CFTC, the last federal functional regulator to sign an information-sharing MOU with FinCEN, had no agreed-upon formal mechanism by which to coordinate or share information with FinCEN until the MOU was finalized in January 2009. CFTC officials stated they approached FinCEN about developing an MOU in fall 2004. CFTC and FinCEN cited delays on the part of both parties in moving forward with the MOU.

In fall 2008, CFTC officials said that they developed standard procedure s for obtaining BSA/AML examination information from its SROs in anticipation of the MOU's finalization. Specifically, CFTC developed templates that identify the episodic, quarterly, and annual report data that will be required to be reported under the MOU and already had rec eived reports from its SROs as of fall 2008. Previously, CFTC did not compile BSA/AML examination statistics, including information on the types of violations cited. Further, FinCEN officials said that CFTC's SROs have not provided their examination modules and procedures to FinCEN but they intended to do so after an MOU with CFTC is finalized.

Without an MOU in place, CFTC's and FinCEN's abilities to evaluate BSA/AML compliance in the futures industry were limite d. For example, without examination procedures and data, similar to that provided by other regulators, FinCEN was not able to evaluate the extent to which BSA/AML regulations were being examined consistently in the futures industry in relation to other sectors. Further, without such information , FinCEN and CFTC were not able to jointly determine areas of BSA compliance weakness and better target guidance or outreach efforts. According to best practices for collaboration, federal agencies engaged in collaborative efforts should create the means to monitor, evaluate, and report their efforts. FinCEN and CFTC officials recognized the benefit s of an MOU and developed information-sharing and data access MOUs (see later discussion on data access) that were completed in January 2009.

IRS and FinCEN Are Discussing Methods to Improve Coordination under Their MOU

While some improvements have been made, FinCEN and IRS disagree on aspects of their MOU and are discussing methods to improve coordination. IRS officials said they asked to renegotiate the terms of the MOU as they said that receive very little benefit from their MOU with FinCEN but that FinCEN has declined, saying the MOU is only 3 years old. However, FinCEN officials said they are in frequent communication with IRS regarding the operation of their MOU and provided documentation of some of these meetings. IRS officials said they believe some of the information they are asked to collect and provide under the MOU is of little use to FinCEN. For example, IRS officials did not think FinCEN made use of IRS's reports of the numbers of Form 8300 and Report of Foreign Bank Account examinations and violations.[64]

According to IRS officials, FinCEN has not held a formal meeting with IRS to discuss the implementation of the MOU, as required by the MOU. However, FinCEN officials stated they have frequent meetings with IRS staff on improving various aspects of BSA administration and information- sharing processes under the MOU. For example, due to recent meetings with FinCEN, IRS officials said that FinCEN improved its time frames for providing responses in cases when IRS officials send FinCEN technical questions they have about BSA compliance in their supervised entities.

FinCEN has taken Steps to Assess Effectiveness of MOUs

FinCEN officials said that in creating their 2008–20 12 strategic plan, they revised goals and performance measures to respond to an assessment and recommendations from the Office of Management and Budget.[65] For fiscal year 2006, the Office of Management and Budget rated Treasury's BSA administration as "results not demonstrated," and FinCEN received low ratings for developing outcome-based performance measures and achieving program results. In fiscal year 2007, a FinCEN working group examined what would constitute meaningful performance measure s for the BSA program.

The working group developed an MOU compliance metric, which measures how effectively MOU holders believe their MOUs facilitate information exchange. In 2008, FinCEN completed a survey of customer perceptions of the services it provides to the federal and state agencie s with which it has information-sharing MOUs. Using results from multiple survey questions, FinCEN staff stated they created a public performance measure and calculated that 64 percent of MOU holders surveyed found FinCEN's information sharing valuable in improving regulatory consistency and compliance in the financial system.[66] FinCEN has set a goal of increasing results for this measure by 2 percentage points annually. Through the survey, FinCEN officials said they also obtained 26 written comments, 14 of which offered suggestions for improving information- sharing MOUs (for example, by providing more communication and feedback).

FinCEN has been Improving Analytical Products; However, Lack of Direct Electronic Access to BSA Data may Limit Compliance Activities

FinCEN has taken steps to improve analytical products for regulators to assist them with their BSA/AML compliance efforts and has been discussing additional products. While some regulators have direct electronic access to BSA data, others have access only through other agencies. For example, FINRA conducts the vast majority of broker-dealer examinations and does not have direct electronic access to BSA data; instead, it must go through FinCEN or SEC to obtain data. FinCEN officials said they finalized a regulatory data-access template in July 2008 and have begun providing additional state regulators with direct electronic access, and anticipate providing expanded access to the federal financial regulators. A FinCEN official said that they are working on data-access MOUs for SROs.

FinCEN has Provided More BSA Data Analyses and has been Discussing Additional Products with Regulators

Under their information-sharing MOUs, FinCEN is to provide analytical products to regulators. As it collects and manages all BSA-related data, FinCEN is in an optimal position to produce analytical products that assess BSA-related issues within and among financial sectors and regulators. FinCEN classifies the analytical reports it produces for its stakeholders into two categories: reactive and proactive. As discussed earlier, FinCEN conducts targeted financial institution analyses for regulators at their request. These analyses are considered reactive reports. As of September 2008, FinCEN's proactive reports included strategic BSA data assessments, "By the Numbers" reports (such as its SAR reports), state-specific BSA data profiles, and reports of possible unregistered and unlicensed MSBs (produced for IRS).

FinCEN stated that the issues for which it chooses to conduct "strategic BSA data assessments" ary. For example, FinCEN officials said it produced a residential real estate assessment after it produced an initial report on commercial real estate as a possible venue for money laundering. FinCEN also conducted an assessment of mortgage fraud after its Office of Regulatory Analysis observed a spike in SAR filings related to mortgage loan fraud. FinCEN officials said that it takes about 4-6 months to produce such assessments, but that they expect this time would be significantly shortened after FinCEN's planned modernization of the BSA database.[67] While the reports are not produced on a regular schedule, FinCEN officials said that it has at least one assessment underway at all times.

FinCEN also biannually produces "By the Numbers" public reports that compile numerical data from SARs and supplement the "SAR Activity Review—Tips, Trends, and Issues" and state-specific BSA data profiles showing analysis of BSA filing trends within the 46 states agencies with which FinCEN has information-sharing MOUs. FinCEN began producing "State BSA Data Profiles" in May 2007 and said it had received input and some positive feedback from state and federal banking regulators. Moreover, some industry officials told us that these publicly available SAR reviews were very useful components of FinCEN's outreach efforts.

In 2008, FinCEN, after discussions with SEC, began providing SEC with reports of securities-related SARs filed by depository institutions. The purpose of these reports is to alert SEC to any possible securities violations observed by depository institutions. To compile the reports, FinCEN analysts search on key terms provided by SEC. SEC staff said they have found these downloads very useful to their general enforcement and examination programs.

Approximately each quarter since June 2006, FinCEN has issued reports on possible unregistered and unlicensed MSBs (found by reviewing SARs filed by depository institutions). IRS officials have used the information to contact and register previously unregistered MSBs. IRS officials also telephone the unregistered MSBs to make sure the entities understand their BSA obligations.

Despite the provision of more analyses, most MOU holders with whom we spoke thought different or additional FinCEN analysis would be useful for their BSA compliance activities and have been discussing such products with FinCEN. In particular, some federal banking regulators said that the summary reports of numbers of examinations, violations, and enforcement actions among depository institutions that FinCEN provides them on a quarterly basis were of little use as they were compilations of data the federal banking regulators had given FinCEN. Although FinCEN provides analyses of issues after reviewing data and reports, federal banking regulator officials thought it would be more beneficial to receive analytical information to assist them in examination preplanning and scoping processes, which would allow them to better focus their BSA/AML resources and efforts. Federal banking regulators have cited requests regarding additional analysis made to FinCEN through the FFIEC BSA/AML working group. For instance, several federal banking regulators have requested state, regional, and national analysis of CTRs and SARs by type of institution, and additional analysis of MSBs and 314(a) hits.[68] As they have limited access to BSA data, federal banking regulators are unable to conduct these analyses themselves. (We discuss data access issues in the following section.) IRS officials said they wanted reports similar to what FinCEN provides to law enforcement, such as analyses of potential money laundering regarding the U.S. southwest border. IRS officials said such reports would be helpful in determining where to allocate the agency's examination resources. FinCEN officials said that they provide IRS (along with the federal banking regulators) a consolidated package containing the annual BSA data profiles for all states and certain U.S. territories. SEC staff they have had at least two discussions with FinCEN staff about analytic products that FinCEN could provide and they expected further discussions would take place.

FinCEN officials stated they needed to concentrate on providing products that could benefit multiple agencies to ensure they were using FinCEN resources effectively. As part of its efficiency and effectiveness initiative, FinCEN said it has identified ways it could increase its analytical support to regulators by providing products with useful information on macro-level risks. FinCEN officials said they are incorporating steps into its information technology modernization plans that will make the development of these products more feasible. FinCEN said it has been developing analyses of 3 14(a) hits to better inform regulators. In addition, one federal banking regulator and FinCEN have agreed to different approaches for obtaining supplemental BSA data analysis. In fall 2008, FDIC officials completed arrangements to have an FDIC analyst work at FinCEN on a part-time basis and that analyst began work with the Office of Regulatory Analysis. FinCEN officials said that they are open to detailees from more regulators as it would also help them understand better which types of analysis are more useful to the regulators.

Regulators have Different Levels of Direct Access to BSA Data, which Inhibits Some Compliance Activities

With the exception of IRS, which maintains and stores all BSA information filed, FinCEN has developed data-access MOUs with some financial regulators to provide them with direct electronic access to BSA data. However, the level of access across financial regulators is inconsistent and has inhibited agencies' compliance activities. For example, FinCEN provides the federal banking regulators with access to CTRs for depository institutions, SARs for depository institutions, and other reports.[69] Federal banking regulators access this information through a secure system but are limited to downloading a certain number of records at a time. Officials from some federal banking regulators said that access to SARs or CTRs filed by institutions other than depository institutions would be useful. One official explained that some institutions, while regulated by others, can be affiliated with their supervised institutions. For example, an MSB may file a SAR on a bank's customer, but the federal banking regulator does not have access to the SAR filed by the MSB. Unlike other federal banking regulators, OCC officials arranged with FinCEN to receive SAR data directly. For about 5 years, OCC has received a monthly compact disc with SAR data for the banks it regulates. With these data, OCC created the "SAR Data Mart," which its staff use to take action against unlawful activity committed by depository institution insiders and for evaluating operational risk. OCC staff have found the ability to conduct is own analyses very useful.

SEC staff said they use their direct access to BSA data to review approximately 100 to 150 SARs for securities and futures firms daily. Furthermore, SEC staff said their access to these SARs has expanded their SAR review activities and enhanced SEC's enforcement and examination programs.

In contrast, futures and securities SROs (including FINRA) and some state agencies that conduct BSA/AML examinations currently do not have direct electronic access to BSA data. Some of these regulators' requests for such access have been pending for several years. FINRA—which conducts the majority of broker-dealer examinations (more than 2,000 in fiscal year 2008)—does not have direct electronic access to BSA data and must request SARs through SEC and FinCEN. With direct electronic access, FINRA and state agency officials told us they could more effectively risk scope their examination processes. Risk scoping by regulators may include reviewing the number of SARs and CTRs filed by institutions under their supervision to identify areas within an institution's program or which institutions among their supervised entities on which to concentrate, enabling regulators to better plan their examinations and target their resources accordingly. As discussed above, federal banking regulators use BSA data to risk scope their examinations. Further, due to the large number of examinations they conduct, FINRA officials said it would strain SEC's resources if FINRA asked SEC staff for access to every SAR filed by the institution under review. Therefore, FINRA staff request SARs from FinCEN primarily when FINRA staff suspect a firm may not have filed all the SARs it says it filed. FINRA officials said they often experienced delays in receiving the information. They also said they started to develop an MOU with FinCEN in 2002; however, the last time FINRA discussed data access with FinCEN was in March 2006.

CFTC is the last federal functional regulator to be provided direct electronic access to the BSA database. CFTC officials said that they made a formal request for direct access to BSA data in 2005. FinCEN officials said that, until recently, FinCEN and CFTC had not agreed on the terms of an electronic access MOU for BSA data. FinCEN and CFTC signed a data-access MOU concurrently with their information-sharing MOU in January 2009. Previously, if CFTC wanted BSA information, it had to make case-by-case requests to FinCEN. Similar to FINRA, CFTC officials said while FinCEN responded quickly to emergency BSA data requests, nonemergency requests could take much longer. CFTC officials said that the data-access MOU will permit CFTC to make BSA database inquiries in certain circumstances on behalf of an SRO. They said that they recognize the unique and highly sensitive nature of BSA data and providing the SROs with direct access to BSA data presents certain legal and regulatory oversight issues.

FinCEN explained it has been conducting a comprehensive evaluation of data access issues. In September 2008, FinCEN completed a bureau-wide initiative to better define the types of regulatory agencies to which it will provide electronic BSA data access and the criteria and processes for evaluating data access requests. FinCEN determined it would consider requests from agencies that examine for BSA compliance; supervise a financial institution for safety and soundness or financial responsibility; issue licenses or charters to financial institutions; or administer or enforce laws, regulations, or rules affecting financial institutions or markets. In evaluating these requests, FinCEN officials said that staff look at the requester's regulatory authorities, ability to protect sensitive BSA data, and ability to utilize confidential information. But they said that SROs present unique issues because of their status as private actors, rather than governmental authorities. Although FinCEN said it anticipates providing SROs with access to appropriate data, their nongovernmental status requires FinCEN to contemplate appropriate access restrictions. FinCEN officials said they finalized a regulatory data-access template in July 2008 and have begun providing additional state regulators with direct electronic access, and anticipate providing expanded access to the federal financial regulators. A FinCEN official said that they are working on data-access MOUs for SROs.

Without electronic access to BSA data, some regulators cannot effectively scope risks for examinations, affecting their ability to efficiently plan examinations and target limited resources to areas of greatest risk. In addition, without direct access, in accordance with their examination procedures they cannot verify information that institutions are reporting on their BSA filings without requesting this information from FinCEN or another regulator who has access, thereby straining already limited resources. For example, as discussed above, to obtain access to some SARs, some regulators (such as FINRA) must contact FinCEN for access, further expending FinCEN's and their limited resources.

CONCLUSIONS

Through the USA PATRIOT Act, more activities of a larger number of financial institutions have come under the umbrella of U.S. anti-money laundering efforts. As the BSA regulation framework has expanded, it also has become more complex—making it all the more important that FinCEN and the regulators establish effective communication and information exchanges to achieve their common goals. While the regulators take different approaches to examination and enforcement within their jurisdictions, they all have responsibilities in the BSA/AML regulatory framework. Additional AML legislation has increased the number of financial institutions that have come under the scope of BSA, as well as regulators' interactions on these issues within and across their respective financial sectors. At the time of our 2006 report, the federal banking regulators and FinCEN already had achieved agreement on how to address some key aspects of BSA compliance and enforcement and developed a common examination manual.

Since that report, FinCEN and the regulators have made additional progress in ensuring the soundness of the current compliance and enforcement framework. While many improvements in the coordination among stakeholders—FinCEN, regulators, law enforcement, and the industries being regulated—have occurred, other working relationships among the stakeholders are not as efficient and effective as they could be. IRS has not fully leveraged its resources with those of state regulators to conduct examinations of MSBs. As a result of IRS not sharing its examination schedules with state agencies, state agency officials told us they sometimes have scheduled examinations shortly after IRS had completed examinations on the same institutions, subjecting them to duplicative monitoring. With approximately 200,000 MSBs in the United States, better coordination of examination scheduling between IRS and its state agency partners would both better leverage limited government resources and minimize the burden placed on those being regulated. Additionally, ongoing meetings such as those of BSAAG provide for some exchange of information, but some important regulatory issues cannot be discussed at meetings at which industry is present. While it is useful to have forums in which the regulators and the regulated exchange information, the sensitive nature of some BSA issues and the nonpublic nature of some examination modules suggest that an additional forum for regular information exchange among all the regulators is called for. Whether it is coordination of efforts between IRS and state regulators or among federal regulators, opening additional avenues for collaboration can (1) facilitate the exchange of best practices and better leverage limited regulatory resources, (2) minimize the regulatory burden on those being regulated, and (3) most importantly, see that the critical concerns embodied in BSA legislation are efficiently and effectively carried out.

FinCEN has taken many significant steps to improve execution of its BSA administrative and coordination responsibilities, but could make improvements in three areas: sharing information with CFTC, improving communication on IRS referrals and ensuring timely feedback to IRS- examined institutions, and reconciling outstanding data access issues. FinCEN also serves as the BSA data manager and provides the regulators with access to critical BSA data related to their supervised entities. With these data, regulators are able to scope risks for their examinations, better target their resources, and independently verify BSA data filings. However, CFTC only received electronic access in January 2009, and securities and futures SROs, and some state agencies do not yet have electronic access to BSA data. With today's rapidly changing financial markets and the relationship of the futures industry to other sectors of the financial markets, it is especially important that SROs receive electronic access to BSA data to facilitate their examinations. Furthermore, IRS is hampered in carrying out its BSA-related compliance responsibilities because of uncertainties about when FinCEN will take action on IRS's referrals. Since IRS does not have enforcement authority in this area, it is important that IRS and FinCEN develop a process that facilitates communication on IRS referrals. Without timely feedback, MSBs may be allowed to continue operating in violation of BSA statutes. Finally, delays in completing data- access agreements present obstacles to some regulators attempting to carry out their BSA-related responsibilities. While FinCEN is justified in its concerns about sharing very sensitive information, the delay in establishing information-sharing and data-access MOUs with CFTC, and the failure to establish data access MOUs with SROs and some states that also have important BSA-related responsibilities, presents a different set of potential problems, such as incomplete risk-scoping of examinations. While we commend FinCEN and CFTC for finalizing their MOUs, the benefits of the agreements will take some time to be realized. Until then, the potential ramifications include less assurance on the part of regulators that these financial institutions are complying fully with the BSA. Taking steps to resolve these areas of concern could provide tangible benefits in the BSA-related efforts of the regulators and build on recent improvements that FinCEN has made in its administrative and coordination responsibilities.

Recommendations for Executive Action

To reduce the potential for duplicative efforts and better leverage limited examination resources, we recommend that the Commissioner of IRS work with state agencies to develop a process by which to coordinate MSB examination schedules between IRS and state agencies that conduct BSA examinations of MSBs.

Further, to build on improvements made in examination processes vital to ensuring BSA compliance, we recommend that the heads of FinCEN, the Federal Reserve, FDIC, OTS, OCC, NCUA, SEC, CFTC, and IRS direct the appropriate staff to consider developing or using an existing process to share and discuss information on BSA/AML examination procedures and general trends regularly in a nonpublic setting. We recommend that the heads of SEC and CFTC consider including the SROs that conduct BSA examinations.

To improve its efforts to administer BSA, we recommend that the Director of FinCEN expeditiously take the following two actions:

- Work with the Commissioner of IRS to establish a mutually agreed-upon process that facilitates communication on IRS referrals and ensures timely feedback to IRS-examined institutions.
- Finalize data-access MOUs with SROs conducting BSA examinations, and states agencies conducting AML examinations that currently have no direct access to BSA data.

AGENCY COMMENTS AND OUR EVALUATION

We provided a draft of this report to the heads of the Departments of Justice and the Treasury; the Federal Reserve, FDIC, NCUA, OCC, OTS, IRS, SEC, and CFTC. We received written comments from FinCEN, IRS, and all the financial regulators. These comments are summarized below and reprinted in appendixes IV-XII. All of the agencies provided technical comments, which we incorporated into this report, where appropriate.

In its comments, IRS agreed with our recommendation that the IRS commissioner work with state agencies to develop a process by which to coordinate BSA examination schedules. The agency said that actions to address our recommendation already were underway.

In their written responses, all of the agencies agreed with our recommendation that they consider developing a mechanism or using an existing process to conduct regular, nonpublic discussions of BSA examination procedures and general trends to better ensure consistency in the application of BSA. In technical comments, some agencies asked that we be more specific about which component of their agencies should participate in and conduct these discussions. We modified the recommendation language to clarify that the heads of the agencies should direct appropriate staff to undertake these actions. The Federal Reserve commented that such discussions could build on improvements already made in examination processes and that regular discussion of examination procedures and general compliance trends could be beneficial. FDIC agreed that periodic meetings with all federal agencies responsible for BSA compliance could promote consistency and coordination in examination and enforcement approaches and help reduce regulatory burden. OCC commented that a number of groups and processes already existed for sharing information and collaboration and that they would continue to participate in these initiatives and look for opportunities to share their practices and observations. OTS commented that that they would collaborate and that the federal banking agencies and FinCEN have established a number of formal committees and working groups to promote collaboration on BSA issues. SEC agreed that the regulators would benefit from the development of such a mechanism and noted that it planned to attend a meeting in which FinCEN was planning to discuss possible methods for achieving this goal. CFTC commented that it supports all efforts to increase cooperation among regulators in the BSA area and that it would be pleased to participate in discussions that would allow the agency to share experiences and expertise in developing and implementing BSA examination procedures.

In its comments, FinCEN said it concurred with the intent of our recommendations, particularly in regard to expanding information sharing with authorized stakeholders, and hoped to be situated in the future to meet them. The draft report that we sent to the agencies for comment contained a recommendation that FinCEN finalize information-sharing and data-access MOUs with CFTC. These MOUs were signed on January 15, 2009, so we have removed the recommendation from the final report. In its comments, CFTC noted that the MOUs had been signed and said that it believed these two agreements would enhance CFTC's ability to ffectively implement its BSA examination responsibilities. hrough discussions with FinCEN officials and FinCEN technical comments, FinCEN provided us with additional information and data about our draft recommendation on IRS referrals. We subsequently broadened the recommendation language to clarify that FinCEN should work with IRS to develop a process to facilitate communication on referrals and ensure timely feedback to IRS-examined institutions. FinCEN and IRS said they agreed with this modification. Finally, in its comments, SEC also supported our recommendation that FinCEN finalize data-access MOUs with SROs that conduct BSA examinations. SEC noted its view that direct access to BSA data would permit FINRA to more effectively use its AML resources to take a more risk-based approach to identifying firms and areas within a firm's AML program that required examination.

As agreed with your office, unless you publicly announce the contents of this report earlier, we plan no further distribution of this report until 30 days from the report date. At that time, we will send copies to interested congressional committees, Treasury, FinCEN, Federal Reserve, FDIC, OCC, OTS, NCUA, SEC, CFTC, IRS, and Justice. The report also will be available at no charge on the GAO Web site at http://www.gao.gov.

If you or you staff have questions about this report, please contact me at (202) 512–8678 or edwardsj@gao.gov. Contact points for our Offices of Congressional Relations and Public Affairs may be found on the last page of this report. GAO staff who made major contributions to this report are listed in appendix XIII.

Jack E. Edwards
Acting Director, Financial Markets and
Community Investment

APPENDIX I: OBJECTIVES, SCOPE AND METHODOLOGY

Our objectives were to (1) describe how Bank Secrecy Act (BSA) compliance and enforcement efforts are distributed among federal and state regulators, self-regulatory organizations (SRO), and the Financial Crimes Enforcement Network (FinCEN); (2) describe how federal agencies other than FinCEN are implementing their BSA activities and evaluate their coordination efforts; and (3) evaluate how FinCEN is executing its BSA responsibilities and coordinating BSA efforts among the various agencies.

To describe how BSA compliance and enforcement efforts are distributed among federal regulators, SRO, and FinCEN, we reviewed and analyzed authorities established by BSA, the USA PATRIOT Act, and other relevant federal financial and anti-money laundering (AML) legislation. We also reviewed prior GAO and Department of the Treasury (Treasury) Inspector General reports on this issue. In addition, to better understand how BSA/AML authorities were delegated and interrelate with other financial regulatory authorities, we interviewed officials from the federal agencies included in the BSA/AML compliance and enforcement regulatory framework—FinCEN; the federal banking regulators: the Board of Governors of the Federal Reserve System (Federal Reserve), Federal Deposit Insurance Corporation (FDIC), Office of the Comptroller of the Currency (OCC), Office of Thrift Supervision (OTS), and National Credit Union Administration (NCUA); Securities and Exchange Commission (SEC), Commodity Futures Trading Commission (CFTC), and the SROs they regulate; Internal Revenue Service (IRS); and Department of Justice (Justice).

To examine how entities with BSA/AML compliance and enforcement responsibilities implement their BSA activities and evaluate their coordination efforts, we reviewed prior GAO reports; available BSA/AML examination manuals and procedures; other related guidance; reports complied in accordance with FinCEN information-sharing memorandums of understanding (MOU); and data maintained on the numbers of the BSA/AML examinations, violations, and enforcement actions taken in the banking, securities, futures, and IRS-examined industries. Further, we conducted data reliability assessments of BSA/AML-related data and found the information to be reliable for the purposes of this report. In addition, we reviewed quality assurance reviews conducted by the federal banking regulators of their BSA/AML examinations. We interviewed officials from all of the federal agencies and their SROs mentioned above and also spoke with officials from select state financial regulatory agencies to obtain information on their BSA/AML compliance and enforcement activities and how these state agencies coordinate with federal agencies. We selected state regulators to interview on the basis of their geography, the presence of a High Intensity Financial Crime Area in their state, the size and variety of the financial sectors present in their state, the existence of a money services business (MSB) examination program in their state, and whether they were contacted by GAO for a previous BSA/AML-related GAO report in 2006.

With respect to the federal banking regulators and their efforts to ensure BSA compliance among depository institutions, we reviewed the Federal Financial Institutions Examinations Council (FFIEC) BSA/AML interagency examination manual, and GAO staff attended 3 days of training on the manual provided to federal and state bank examiners. We also reviewed quarterly and annual reports which included data on examinations, violations, and enforcement actions, as well as information on staffing and training, that were submitted by the federal banking regulators to FinCEN per their MOU. We reviewed these reports to assess whether regulators were in compliance with MOU requirements and to inform our understanding of their BSA/AML compliance activities. In addition to meetings with federal banking regulator

BSA/AML program staff, we also held interviews with groups of examiners from each of the federal banking regulators to discuss the manual and interagency coordination. We also spoke with a state banking regulatory association and credit union regulatory association. Further, to obtain industry perspective, in cooperation with another GAO team looking at the usefulness of suspicious activity reports (SAR), we interviewed two banking industry associations and 20 depository institutions on the impact of the manual and coordination among federal and state banking regulators.

To select the 20 depository institutions, we grouped the depository institutions into four categories depending on the numbers of SARs filed in calendar year 2007. We interviewed representatives from all 5 institutions that had the largest number of SAR filings in 2007, as well as representatives from 15 randomly selected institutions. The 15 institutions represented different categories of SAR filings: small (1-4 SARs filed in 2007), medium (5-88), and large (more than 88—excluding the 5 largest).

To obtain information on the BSA/AML compliance and enforcement activities of SEC, CFTC, and IRS, we interviewed officials from these agencies, as well as officials from securities and futures SROs; state regulatory agencies; securities and futures firms; and securities, futures, and money transmitter industry associations. We interviewed 8 securities firms through the auspices of an industry trade association and interviewed one large and small futures drawn from a list provided by a futures regulator. In addition, we reviewed available examination modules; related training guidance; and reports provided to FinCEN by SEC and IRS in accordance with their information-sharing MOUs that contain data on BSA/AML examinations, violations, and enforcement actions; as well as BSA/AML training and staffing information. We obtained and reviewed similar information from CFTC. To describe Justice's enforcement actions, we interviewed Justice officials, analyzed Justice's enforcement actions, and reviewed other BSA/AML-related Justice documentation. In order to evaluate coordination efforts, we compared the practices of these agencies with best practices outlined in a GAO report evaluating coordination practices among federal agencies.[70]

To evaluate FinCEN BSA/AML compliance and enforcement efforts, we collected and reviewed available staffing and performance measurement data from FinCEN, program assessments, BSA/AML-violation referral data from its Case Management System (CMS), FinCEN analytical products, strategic plans and annual reports, and other documentation. We also assessed the reliability of data provided to us by FinCEN from its CMS and found it to be reliable for the purposes of this report. In addition, we reviewed the three surveys FinCEN conducted of users of its Regulatory Resource Center in 2006, 2007, and 2008 and a fourth survey it conducted of regulators with which it has information-sharing MOUs. Despite some potential limitations associated with the surveys, we concluded that the overall frequencies for survey questions should be sufficiently valid and reflected the overall opinions of those surveyed. FinCEN officials also told us that information-sharing MOU survey respondents might have, in some cases, been providing responses to reflect their experiences with data- access MOUs. Further, we interviewed FinCEN officials from the Office of the Director, Management Programs Division, the Analysis and Liaison Division, and the Regulatory Policy and Programs Division (RPPD). We conducted interviews with staff from each of the offices within RPPD. In addition, we conducted interviews with officials from the federal banking regulators, SEC, CFTC, securities and futures SROs, IRS, and industry to discuss FinCEN's efforts.

We conducted this performance audit in Washington, D.C., New York, New York, and Chicago, Illinois, from October 2007 to February 2009 in accordance with generally accepted government auditing standards. Those standards require that we plan and perform the audit to obtain sufficient, appropriate evidence to provide a reasonable basis for our findings and conclusions based on our audit objectives. We believe that the evidence obtained provides a reasonable basis for our findings and conclusions based on our audit objectives.

Appendix II: Overview of Federal Agencies Involved in the BSA/AML Framework and Related Resources

This appendix provides an overview of the compliance and enforcement activities of the federal financial regulators and IRS and provides information, to the extent it is available, on their BSA-related resources and training.

Overview of Federal Agencies Involved in BSA/AML Compliance and Enforcement

The federal banking regulators (the Board of Governors of the Federal Reserve System (Federal Reserve), Federal Deposit Insurance Corporation

(FDIC), Office of the Comptroller of the Currency (OCC), Office of Thrift Supervision (OTS), and National Credit Union Administration (NCUA)), Securities Exchange Commission (SEC), Commodity Futures Trading Commission (CFTC), securities and futures self-regulatory organizations (SRO), and Internal Revenue Service (IRS) play roles in implementing BSA/AML compliance. The U.S. regulatory system is described as "functional," so that financial products or activities are generally regulated according to their function, no matter who offers the product or participates in the activity. Below is a discussion of their missions and how they undertake general compliance and enforcement activities within their industries.

Federal Banking Regulators

Depository institutions can generally determine their regulators by choosing a particular kind of charter—for example, commercial bank, thrift, or credit union. These charters may be obtained at the state level or the national level. While state regulators charter institutions and participate in oversight of those institutions, all of these institutions have a primary federal regulator if they have federal deposit insurance. Broadly, the federal banking regulators that provide oversight for banks are the Federal Reserve, FDIC, and OCC; thrifts—OTS; and credit unions— NCUA.[71] Banking regulators generally focus on ensuring the safety and soundness of their supervised institutions. They conduct safety and soundness examinations on-site to assess an institution's financial condition, policies and procedures, and adherence to laws and regulations. Generally, regulatory agencies perform these examinations every 12 to 18 months, based on the institution's risk. The Federal Reserve, FDIC, OTS, and NCUA (but not OCC) alternate or conduct joint safety and soundness examinations with state regulators, generally using the same examination procedures. State banking regulators may examine depository institutions chartered within their jurisdictions.

Federal and state banking regulators may address compliance problems identified through their examinations by bringing the problem to the attention of institution management and obtaining a commitment to take corrective action. When these actions are insufficient or weaknesses identified are more substantive, regulators may take nonpublic, informal enforcement actions. Informal actions (which vary among the federal banking regulators) may include the adoption of resolutions by an institution's board of directors, the execution of a memorandums of understanding between an institution and the regulators, notices of safety and soundness deficiency for compliance, commitment letters, or corrective actions to be taken to address regulatory concerns. Informal actions usually are taken to address violations that are limited in scope and technical in nature. Federal banking regulators also may take formal enforcement actions if a depository institution is engaging in unsafe or unsound practices or has violated a law or regulation. Formal enforcement actions are public and generally considered more stringent than informal actions and can address more significant, repeated, or systemic BSA violations. Formal enforcement actions include cease-and-desist orders, assessments of civil money penalties (CMP), or supervisory agreements. These types of actions are enforceable through an administrative process or injunctive relief in federal district court.

SEC and Securities SROs

SEC's mission is to protect investors; maintain fair, orderly, and efficient securities markets; and facilitate capital formation. SEC regulates the securities industry in part through oversight of its SROs. SEC, through its Office of Compliance and Examination (OCIE) shares examination responsibilities with securities SROs, which include examining for BSA/AML compliance. OCIE's routine examinations are conducted according to a cycle that is based on a registrant's perceived risk. In addition to routine examinations, OCIE also may conduct sweep examinations to probe specific activities of a sample of firms to identify emerging compliance problems so they can be remedied before becoming severe or systemic. Third, OCIE conducts cause examinations when it has reason to believe that something is wrong at a particular firm.

SROs have statutory responsibilities to regulate their own members, and one SRO—the Financial Industry Regulatory Association (FINRA)—provides oversight of the majority of broker-dealers in the securities industry. SROs conduct risk-based examinations, which include a BSA component, of their members to ensure compliance with SRO rules and federal securities laws. These examinations are conducted on a risk-based cycle (similar to SEC's), and no member is examined less frequently than every 4 years.

Through oversight inspections of the SROs, OCIE evaluates the quality of the SROs' oversight in enforcing member compliance. At regular intervals, OCIE conducts routine inspections of SROs' key regulatory programs, such as SRO enforcement, arbitration, and examination programs. Inspection of enforcement programs typically includes a review of SRO surveillance programs for identifying potential violations of trading rules or laws, investigating those potential violations, and disciplining those who violate the rule or law.

SEC and its SROs also have enforcement divisions that are responsible for investigating and prosecuting violations of securities laws or regulations as identified through examinations; referrals from other regulatory organizations; and tips from firm insiders, the public, and other sources. For less significant issues, examiners may cite a deficiency for correction through remedial actions. SEC and SRO examiners conduct exit interviews with firms, which are usually followed by letters discussing examination findings. SEC issues deficiency letters that formally identify compliance failures or internal control weaknesses at a firm.[72] Most examinations conclude with the firm voluntarily correcting the compliance problem and stating the specific actions it is taking in its response to SEC. Potential SEC enforcement sanctions include disgorgement, CMPs, cease-and-desist orders, and injunctions. When SROs find evidence of potential violations of securities laws or SRO rules by their members, they can conduct disciplinary hearings and impose penalties. These penalties can range from disciplinary letters to the imposition of monetary fines to expulsion from trading and SRO membership.

CFTC and Futures SROs

CFTC's primary mission is to preserve the integrity of the futures markets and protect market users and the public from fraud, manipulation, and abusive practices related to the sale of commodity futures and options.

While CFTC directly performs the market surveillance and enforcement functions, CFTC carries out its regulatory functions with respect to futures firms through SROs that act as the primary supervisor for members of the futures industry. CFTC does not routinely conduct direct examinations of the institutions that it supervises; instead, it oversees their SROs'—the National Futures Association (NFA), Chicago Mercantile Exchange, New York Mercantile Exchange, Chicago Board of Trade, and the Kansas City Board of Trade—examinations of futures firms. Each futures exchange is an SRO that governs its floor brokers, traders, and member firms. NFA also regulates every firm or individual that conducts futures trading business with public customers. SROs are responsible for establishing and enforcing rules governing member conduct and trading, providing for the prevention of market manipulation, ensuring futures industry professionals meet qualifications, and examining exchange members for financial soundness and other regulatory purposes. SROs examine their members for compliance with their rules, including those imposing BSA/AML requirements. The futures SROs' examination cycles range from 9 to 18 months for futures commission merchants, but introducing brokers may have longer examination cycles.

While CTFC does not conduct routine examinations of futures firms, it provides oversight of futures SROs to ensure that each has an effective self-regulatory program. CFTC's Division of Clearing and Intermediary Oversight conducts periodic, risk-based examinations of an SRO's compliance examination program, which may include BSA/AML issues. During the examination, CFTC reviews the SRO's documentation of select examinations and independently performs examinations for the same periods to compare its results with those of the SRO's examinations.

SROs may take enforcement actions against any member that is in violation of member rules and CFTC regulations, which include BSA/AML-related rules. BSA/AML obligations for the futures industry are set forth in the USA PATRIOT Act, BSA, FinCEN and CTFC regulations, and SRO member rules. CFTC's Division of Enforcement investigates and prosecutes alleged violations of the Commodity Exchange Act and CFTC regulations, and reviews SRO open investigations and enforcement actions.

IRS

IRS is a bureau within Treasury, with the mission of helping taxpayers understand and meet their tax responsibilities and ensuring that all taxpayers comply with tax laws. Unlike others with BSA/AML compliance responsibilities, IRS does not conduct examinations of compliance with any legislation other than BSA/AML rules and regulations. FinCEN delegated BSA examination authority to IRS for any financial institution not subject to BSA examination by another federal regulator. These institutions are mainly nonbank financial institutions (NBFI) such as casinos, some credit unions, credit card operators, and approximately 200,000 money service businesses (MSB), which are the most numerous of the NBFIs.

IRS's Small Business/Self-Employed Division, which reports to the Deputy Commissioner of Services and Employment, conducts BSA compliance examinations of NBFIs. In 2004, IRS created the Office of BSA/Fraud within the Small Business/Self-Employed Division to better focus on BSA examinations of NBFIs. IRS's BSA program also aims to increase the number of identified NBFIs, conduct outreach and education to NBFIs, and refer any NBFIs to the Financial Crimes Enforcement Network (FinCEN) or IRS Criminal Investigation for civil and criminal enforcement actions. IRS Criminal Investigation, IRS's enforcement arm, investigates individuals and businesses suspected of criminal violations of the Internal Revenue Code, money laundering and currency crime, and some BSA laws. IRS Criminal Investigation usually investigates BSA criminal violations in conjunction with other tax violations. IRS Criminal Investigation's first enforcement priority is tax fraud and tax evasion, but currency reporting and money laundering enforcement also are areas of emphasis.

Federal Agencies Generally Incorporate BSA/AML-related Staffing and Training into Overall Compliance Programs, but Some Maintain BSA/AMLdedicated Information on Resources

Staffing

The federal banking regulators, SEC, and CFTC incorporate their BSA activities into their overall compliance programs. However, all the regulators either track the number of hours spent on BSA/AML issues or numbers of staff with BSA/AML-related responsibilities. All of the regulators have staff that examine institutions for BSA/AML compliance concurrently with their comprehensive safety and soundness compliance examinations. The points below summarize BSA/AML-specific data (for 2008 where possible) for each regulator (IRS excepted):

- *Federal Reserve*. The Federal Reserve has a BSA/AML Risk Section within its Division of Banking Supervision and Regulation, which consists of seven staff who monitor BSA/AML compliance concerns and liaise with staff from Federal Reserve Banks to provided guidance on BSA/AML issues. Federal Reserve officials said they also have BSA/AML specialists located in some Federal Reserve Banks.

- *FDIC*. In 2008, of the 1,680 examiners that conduct safety and soundness examination (during which a BSA/AML examination is conducted concurrently), 324 were BSA subject matter experts, and 117 are certified AML specialist examiners. Further, FDIC officials estimated the agency devoted 107.4 and 103.5 full-time equivalent positions to BSA/AML activities in 2006 and 2007, respectively.

- *OCC*. OCC has a Director for BSA/AML Compliance that oversees a staff of six full-time BSA/AML compliance specialists in its headquarters. From 2005 through 2007, OCC officials estimated that the agency annually devoted an average of 105 full-time equivalent positions to the BSA, while in 2008, OCC devoted approximately 86 full-time equivalents.

- *OTS.* In 2008, OTS reported that five Regional Assistant Directors for Compliance serve as subject matter resources on BSA, in addition to 15 regional compliance specialists, and 2 national office staff that are dedicated to BSA/AML issues. OTS officials estimated the time its attorneys devoted to BSA/AML issues as being equivalent to two full-time positions.

- *NCUA.* As of September 30, 2008, NCUA reported employing 514 examiners, which included 31 examiners designated as consumer compliance subject matter examiners (which includes BSA/AML issues). Each of NCUA's five regional offices has at least one BSA/AML analyst, its Office of Examination and Insurance has two BSA/AML program officers, and the Office of General Counsel has two attorneys that focus on BSA issues.

- *SEC.* SEC has a BSA/AML team comprised of from five to seven OCIE staff members, from three to five Division of Enforcement staff members, and three members from the Division of Trading and Markets. The team is responsible for monitoring its BSA/AML examination program; providing expertise to regional offices; and maintaining communication with FinCEN, the SROs, and other regulators on AML issues. Further, SEC broker-dealer examination staff have an AML working group consisting of one or more representatives from each regional office, who serve as AML experts. FINRA has nine AML regulatory experts.

- *CFTC.* CFTC does not have full-time staff dedicated solely to BSA/AML compliance; however, various staff may be involved in BSA/AML issues. CFTC staff conduct periodic oversight examinations of SROs' compliance examination programs, which include a review of BSA/AML procedures. CFTC staff also devote time to BSA/AML policy issues during the rule-making process and at other times, as requested by FinCEN. Futures SROs include BSA/AML as part of their broader compliance examination programs. NFA and the Chicago Mercantile Exchange have 130 and 59 examination staff respectively, all of which have been trained in BSA/AML.

Training

All of the regulators and their SROs that examine financial institutions for BSA/AML compliance provide opportunities to their staff to receive BSA/AML training—provided by the agency, working groups (such as FFIEC), or outside vendors. FFIEC, for example, provides both an AML workshop for examiners knowledgeable of BSA and experienced in examining institutions for BSA program compliance and, as of 2007, an advanced BSA/AML specialists conference for designated BSA compliance examiners and other BSA subject matter experts. In 2007, over 400 trainees participated in these programs. Agencies and SROs provided several examples of BSA/AML training available to their staff and others (see table 11).

IRS has a BSA/AMLSpecific Compliance Unit, Budget, and Performance Measures

Unlike the federal banking regulators, SEC, and CFTC, who incorporate BSA activities into their compliance programs, IRS's BSA/AML activities are managed separately in its Office of Fraud/BSA within the Small Business/Self Employment division. This office is solely dedicated to examining NFBIs for BSA compliance. Since IRS created the office, IRS has tracked several BSA-specific output and efficiency performance measures, such as number of examinations, referrals, closures, and hours per case (see table 12). IRS also has a detailed strategic plan devoted to BSA compliance and enforcement activities.

We previously reported that IRS lacked a measure for NBFI compliance rates with BSA and thus could not track program effectiveness over time. We recommended that the Secretary of Treasury direct FinCEN and IRS to develop a documented and coordinated strategy—that would include priorities, time frames, and resource needs, and measure the compliance rate of NBFIs—to improve BSA compliance by NBFIs.[73] IRS and FinCEN responded by developing such a strategy, which identifies various NBFI categories, prioritizes actions to be taken overall and within each category for improving BSA compliance, explains who is responsible for the actions, and establishes the time frames for identifying whether an action has been completed or when it is to be completed. Similar to the other regulators, IRS's Office of BSA/Fraud conducts quality reviews of examinations.

Over the last several years, IRS has increased the resources it devotes to BSA compliance. In fiscal year 2007, IRS spent over $71 million and 700 full-time equivalents on BSA-related activities, which is an increase of 3 percent and 5 percent, respectively, from 2006. Specifically, the Small Business/Self Employment's Office of Fraud/BSA increased its BSA field examiner staff from 372 in 2006 to 385 in 2007. New Small Business/Self Employment employees receive Basic BSA/AML training on both BSA and currency transaction reporting requirements (Form 8300 examinations). Experienced BSA examiners receive specialized training for specific industries, such as insurance companies, credit unions, casinos, and jewelry and precious metals dealers. IRS also has developed specific BSA training for managers and coaches of BSA examiners. The Office of Fraud/BSA also distributes a BSA/AML examination guide, provides BSA newsletters, and updated the Insurance Industry Guide and Internal Revenue Manual.

APPENDIX III: EXAMPLES OF BSA/AML-RELATED FORMAL ENFORCEMENT ACTIONS

In fiscal year 2008, approximately 70 BSA/AML-related formal enforcement actions were taken by federal financial regulators--the Board of Governors of the Federal Reserve System (Federal Reserve), Federal Deposit Insurance Corporation (FDIC), Office of the Comptroller of the Currency (OCC), Office of Thrift Supervision (OTS), Securities Exchange Commission (SEC)--the National Futures Association (NFA), the Financial Industry Regulatory Authority (FINRA), and other self-regulatory organizations (SROs). In fiscal years 2006-2008, the Financial Crimes Enforcement Network (FinCEN) and the federal financial regulators and SROs jointly assessed 11 civil money penalties (CMP). Table 13 contains examples of formal enforcement actions, excluding CMPs, that were not taken concurrently with FinCEN.

Table 14 lists examples of BSA/AML-related CMPs issued: (1) jointly by federal and state regulators, SROs, and FinCEN; (2) solely by FinCEN; and (3) by federal regulators only.

Table 11. BSA/AML Training, by Regulator

Regulators and SROs	Training description
Federal Reserve	Federal Reserve staff conduct BSA/AML training using an online training module. The Federal Reserve's BSA/AML Risk Section conducts monthly telephone calls and hosts two conferences each year with senior BSA/AML staff.
FDIC	FDIC offers a certificate program for FDIC personnel on the BSA/AML examination process. FDIC also trains its legal and consumer compliance staff on BSA/AML; FDIC officials added that once every 3 years, each regional office has mandatory examiner training conferences that include BSA issues. Further, every 18 months, FDIC holds a joint conference with the Department of Justice (Justice) that focuses on fraud aspects of AML that state bank regulators also attend.
OCC	Among its training initiatives, OCC has online training, an "AML School," and provides additional training opportunities through external conferences. The "AML School" is a 27-hour classroom course, which is designed to train participants to recognize potential money laundering risks, including suspicious activity monitoring, and assess the adequacy of an institution's policies and procedures.
OTS	OTS provides BSA/AML training to its examiners through internal and external conferences, as well as meeting and online training modules. It includes BSA/AML compliance in its advanced compliance examiner schools.
NCUA	NCUA officials said that part of its core examiner training addresses BSA, and they also provide BSA training at the Consumer Compliance SME conferences. Examiners also obtain BSA training from external sources.
SEC	SEC regularly trains staff on BSA, including joint training with the SROs. SEC recently conducted a 3-day training session with its SROs that focused on AML. FinCEN, Office of Foreign Assets Control, High Intensity Financial Crime Area, and SRO staff were among the speakers.[a]
FINRA	FINRA provides its examiners with training through BSA/AML-specific online learning and telephone-in workshops, as well as Internet broadcasts. In addition, FINRA's "Compliance Boot Camp" has included an AML component, which has been developed into a separate "AML Boot Camp." Further, FINRA holds annual joint trainings with other SROs' examiners on BSA/AML compliance.
CFTC	CFTC periodically trains its staff on BSA, including joint training with the SROs. Most recently, CFTC conducted staff training jointly with NFA. The training covered, among other things, NFA's AML examination protocol as well as certain money laundering hypotheticals.
NFA	New NFA audit staff members receive AML training as part of their initial audit training; and examiners receive ongoing training, updates on regulations, guidance, or notices relating to BSA/AML. NFA's Compliance Department discusses any new AML issues at staff meetings and maintains an intranet page with AML information and staff guidance.

Source: Regulator documentation and data.

[a] The Office of Foreign Assets Control administers and enforces economic and trade sanctions against countries and groups of individuals, such as terrorists and narcotics traffickers. Beginning in 2000, Treasury and Justice designated certain areas as High Intensity Financial Crime Areas: Chicago, Illinois; Los Angeles, California; San Francisco, California; Miami, Florida; San Juan, Puerto Rico; the southwest border (Texas and Arizona); and New York and New Jersey. The designations were designed to allow law enforcement to concentrate resources in areas where money laundering or related financial crimes were occurring at a higher-than-average rate.

Table 12. IRS BSA Performance Measures, Fiscal Years 2004–2007

Performance measure	FY 2004	FY 2005	FY 2006	FY 2007
Number of closures	3,481	3,712	6,538	8,531
Hours per case	[a]	49	40	33
Cycle time	[a]	218	188	132
Case in inventory				
Assigned to examiner— examination not started	[b]	[b]	3,520	2,823
Assigned to examiner— examination started	[b]	[b]	2,707	3,404
Net number of new starts	[b]	[b]	2,664	3,100
Referrals to IRS-CI	9	21	12	24
Referrals to FinCEN	8	10	14	22
Referrals to tax examiners	1,663	1,572	677	[c]

Sources: GAO and IRS.

[a] Information on hours per case and cycle time was not captured until January 2005.

[b] Information is not provided for fiscal years 2004 and 2005.

[c] The methodology for capturing this information has changed and information is not available as a measure comparable to prior fiscal years.

Table 13. Examples of Formal Enforcement Actions, Excluding CMPs, Taken By Federal Financial Regulators and SROs for BSA/AML-related Compliance Problems, Fiscal Years 2006–2008

Enforcement action	Date	Regulator	Other regulators involved in the issuance of the enforcement action	Depository institution	Areas of significant BSA- related problems
Cease-and-desist order	4/2006	FDIC[a]	West Virginia Division of Banking	MCNB Bank and Trust Co.	Internal controls Independent audit Independent testing BSA compliance officer
Cease-and-desist order	8/2006	FDIC		FirstBank of Puerto Rico	BSA compliance program Currency transaction reporting Suspicious activity reporting Customer due diligence
Cease-and-desist order	7/2007	FDIC		Central Prog-ressive Bank	BSA compliance officer BSA compliance program
Cease-and-desist order	4/2008	FDIC		Sun Security Bank	Financial recordkeeping Currency transaction reporting Suspicious activity reporting

Table 13.- (Continued)

Cease-and-desist order	6/2006	Federal Reserve	Missouri Department of Economic Development	Progress Bancshares, Inc.	Independent testing Customer due diligence
Written agreement	3/2007	Federal Reserve	New York State Banking Department	Banco de la Nacion Argentina	BSA compliance program Suspicious activity reporting Customer due diligence Transaction monitoring
Written agreement	3/2007	Federal Reserve	Ohio Division of Financial Institutions	North Valley Bank	Suspicious activity reporting Customer due diligence
Written agreement	1/2008	Federal Reserve	Indiana Department of Financial Institutions	Salin Bank and Trust Company	BSA compliance program Suspicious activity reporting Customer due diligence
Expulsion	4/2006	National Association of Securities Dealers		Salomon Grey Financial Corporation	BSA compliance program Customer identification program Suspicious activity reporting Training Independent testing Internal controls BSA compliance officer
Cease-and-desist order	2/2007	National Credit Union Administration (NCUA)		Dover N.J. Spanish American Federal Credit Union	BSA compliance officer Monitoring wire transfers Currency transaction reporting Suspicious activity reporting Internal controls
Cease-and-desist order	6/2007	NCUA		Garden Savings Federal Credit Union	BSA compliance program BSA compliance officer Customer identification program Customer due diligence Suspicious activity reporting Currency transaction reporting BSA written procedures Training 314(a) requests Independent testing
Complaint	8/2006	NFA		Spencer Financial, LLC	Written AML policies and procedures Customer identification program 314(a) requests Training Independent audit
Complaint	12/2006	NFA		Steadfast Futures Options	Training Suspicious activity reporting Customer identification program Independent audit
Complaint	10/2007	NFA		Edwards Thomas	BSA compliance program Independent audit

				Trading Co.	Training
Complaint	8/2008	NFA		Commodity Futures Consultants Corp.	Monitoring wire transfers Suspicious activity reporting
Written agreement	2/2006	OCC		Maryland Bank and Trust Company, N.A.	BSA compliance program Internal controls Training Financial record keeping BSA compliance officer
Cease-and-desist order	9/2006	OCC		Doha Bank	BSA compliance program Monitoring wire transfers Suspicious activity reporting Internal controls
Written agreement	11/2006	OCC		FirstMerit Bank	BSA compliance officer Internal controls Independent audit Training Monitoring wire transfers
Written agreement	3/2007	OCC		Farmers National Bank of Osborne	BSA compliance program BSA compliance officer Internal controls Independent testing Training Written AML polices and procedures
Written agreement	7/2008	OCC		Granite Community Bank, N.A.	Internal controls Transaction monitoring Monitoring wire transfers Currency transaction reporting Suspicious activity reporting
Written agreement	10/2008	OCC		Omni National Bank	Internal controls Independent testing Customer due diligence Suspicious activity reporting
Written agreement	12/2005	OTS		Baltimore County Savings Bank, FSB	BSA compliance program Customer identification program Written AML policies and procedures Currency transaction reporting
Cease-and-desist order	4/2006	OTS		United Trust Bank	BSA compliance program Internal controls Training Independent testing Suspicious activity reporting Currency transaction reporting Customer identification program
Cease-and-desist order	10/2006	OTS		R-G Crown Bank	BSA compliance program Customer identification program Financial record keeping BSA compliance officer Training Suspicious activity reporting

Table 13.- (Continued)

Written agreement	5/2007	OTS		First Federal Savings and Loan Association of Greensburg	BSA compliance officer Training Independent testing Internal controls Customer identification program Currency transaction reporting Suspicious activity reporting
Cease-and-desist order	10/2007	OTS		Washington Mutual Bank	BSA compliance officer Training Independent testing Internal controls Customer identification program
Cease-and-desist order	5/2006	SEC		Crowell, Weedon & Co.	Customer identification program
Cease-and-desist order	12/2007	SEC		Park Financial Group, Inc.	Suspicious activity reporting
Cease-and-desist order	7/2008	SEC		E*Trade Clearing, LLC and E*Trade Securities, LLC	Customer identification program

Source: GAO analysis of enforcement actions provided by federal regulators and SROs.

Note: FinCEN only issues penalties or notification/warning letters. FinCEN does not take any other administrative actions (such as Cease-and-Desist Orders). Accordingly, regulators are not required to submit notice of many of these actions to FinCEN as they were only partially BSA-related actions.

[a]FDIC issued 7, 29, and 17 formal enforcement actions for BSA/AML-related compliance problems in fiscal years 2006, 2007, and 2008, respectively.

[b]The Federal Reserve issued 8, 7, and 2 formal enforcement actions for BSA-related compliance problems in fiscal years 2006, 2007, and 2008, respectively.

[c]NCUA issued two formal enforcement actions for BSA-related compliance problems in fiscal year 2007.

[d]NFA issued 21, 10, and 8 formal enforcement actions for BSA/AML-related compliance problems in calendar years 2006, 2007, and 2008, respectively. Data for calendar year 2008 is through August 19, 2008.

[e]OCC issued 19, 14, and 9 formal enforcement actions for BSA/AML-related compliance problems in fiscal years 2006, 2007, and 2008, respectively.

[f]OTS issued 15, 13, and 9 formal enforcement actions for BSA/AML-related compliance problems in fiscal years 2006, 2007, and 2008, respectively.

[g]SEC issued 2 formal enforcement actions for BSA/AML-related compliance problems in fiscal year 2008.

Table 14. Examples of CMPs Assessed by FinCEN, Federal Financial Regulators, and SROs for BSA/AML-related Compliance Violations, Fiscal Years 2006–2008

Date	Financial institution or other party	CMP amount	CMP assessed jointly by FinCEN and the designated examining authority	Designated examining authority with whom FinCEN jointly assessed CMP	CMP assessed solely by FinCEN	CMP assessed solely by the federal regulator	Federal designated examining authority
10/2005	Banco de Chile- New York and Banco de Chile- Miami	$3,000,000	X	OCC			Federal Reserve and OCC
12/2005	The New York branch of ABN AMRO Bank N.V.	80,000,000	X	Federal Reserve, New York State Banking Department			Federal Reserve
12/2005	Oppenheimer & Co, Inc.	2,800,000	X	New York Stock Exchange			SEC
3/20006	The Tonkawa Tribe of Oklahoma and Edward E. Street	1,000,000 and 1,500,000			X		Internal Revenue Service (IRS)
4/2006	Home Building and Loan Company	15,000				X	OTS
4/2006	The New York Branch of Metropolitan Bank and Trust Company	150,000	X	OCC			OCC
4/2006	BankAtlantic	10,000,000[a]	X	OTS			OTS
5/2006	Frosty Food Mart	10,000			X		IRS
5/2006	Liberty Bank of New York	600,000	X	FDIC, New York State Banking Department			FDIC
7/2006	Deprez's Quality Jewelry and Loans, Inc.	25,000			X		IRS
10/2006	Israeli Discount Bank of New York	12,000,000	X	FDIC, New York State Banking Department			FDIC
12/2006	The Foster Bank	2,000,000			X		FDIC

Table 14. (Continued)

Date	Financial institution or other party	CMP amount	CMP assessed jointly by FinCEN and the designated examining authority	Designated examining authority with whom FinCEN jointly assessed CMP	CMP assessed solely by FinCEN	CMP assessed solely by the federal regulator	Federal designated examining authority
12/2006	Beach Bank	800,000	X	FDIC, Florida Office of Financial Regulation			FDIC
2/2007	International Bank of Miami	250,000				X	OCC
5/2007	United Bank of Africa, Plc	500,000				X	OCC
8/2007	American Express Bank International and American Express Travel Related Services Company, Inc.	20,000,000 and 5,000,000[b]	X	Federal Reserve			Federal Reserve
9/2007	Union Bank of California, N.A.	10,000,000[c]	X	OCC			OCC
1/2008	Sigue Corporation and Sigue, LLC	12,000,000[d]			X		IRS
4/2008	El Noa Noa Corporation	12,000			X		IRS
4/2008	NY Branch United Bank of Africa	$15,000,000	X	OCC			OCC

Source: GAO analysis of enforcement actions provided by federal regulators and FinCEN.

[a]CMP issued concurrently with a Justice-deferred prosecution agreement and accompanying $1 0, 000,000 forfeiture.

[b]CMP issued concurrently with a Justice-deferred prosecution agreement and accompanying $55,000,000 forfeiture by Justice and a cease-and-desist order and $20,000,000 CMP by the Federal Reserve.

[c]CMP issued concurrently with a Justice-deferred prosecution agreement and accompanying $21,600,000 forfeiture.

[d]CMP issued concurrently with a Justice-deferred prosecution agreement and accompanying $15,000,000 forfeiture.

APPENDIX IV: COMMENTS FROM THE DEPARTMENT OF THE TREASURY'S FINANCIAL CRIMES ENFORCEMENT NETWORK

DEPARTMENT OF THE TREASURY
FINANCIAL CRIMES ENFORCEMENT NETWORK

DIRECTOR

February 2, 2009

Mr. Jack Edwards
Acting Director, Financial Markets and Community Investment
U.S. Government Accountability Office
441 G Street N.W.
Washington, D.C. 20515

Dear Mr. Edwards:

Thank you for the opportunity to review and comment on the Government Accountability Office (GAO) draft report entitled, *BANK SECRECY ACT: Federal Agencies Should Take Action to Further Improve Coordination and Information-Sharing Efforts.* One of the Department's goals is to promote the nation's security through strengthened financial systems. The Bank Secrecy Act (BSA) contributes to this goal by ensuring that financial activity is safer and more transparent. As administrator of the BSA, the Financial Crimes Enforcement Network (FinCEN) is responsible for ensuring effective, efficient, and consistent application of, examination for, and enforcement of the BSA.

As you know, various industries are subject to the BSA. Authority to examine financial institutions for compliance with the requirements is delegated to the five Federal Banking Agencies, the Securities and Exchange Commission, the Commodity Futures Trading Commission, and the Internal Revenue Service. Each of these agencies refers back to FinCEN indications of significant violations, for FinCEN to consider whether to take an enforcement action under the BSA. Ensuring consistency among such diversity is an ongoing challenge, but a challenge that FinCEN takes seriously and remains committed to improving. I personally have engaged with the leadership of each of the eight aforementioned agencies regarding BSA issues. FinCEN concurs with the intent of the recommendations, particularly in regard to expanding information sharing with authorized stakeholders, and hopes to be situated in the future to meet these suggestions. In addition, FinCEN provided technical comments under separate cover for GAO's consideration in finalizing the audit report.

We appreciate GAO's efforts in reviewing BSA compliance and enforcement. If you have any questions, then please feel free to contact Jamal El-Hindi, Associate Director, Regulatory Policy and Programs Division, at 202-354-6414.

Sincerely,

/s/

James H. Freis, Jr.

www.fincen.gov

Appendix V: Comments from the Internal Revenue Service

DEPARTMENT OF THE TREASURY
INTERNAL REVENUE SERVICE
WASHINGTON, D.C. 20224

DEPUTY COMMISSIONER

February 02, 2009

Mr. Jack Edwards
Acting Director
Financial Markets and Community Investment
U.S. Government Accountability Office
441 G Street, N.W.
Washington, D.C. 20548

Dear Mr. Edwards:

Thank you for the opportunity to review and comment on the Government Accountability Office (GAO) draft report titled, "BANK SECRECY ACT: Federal Agencies Should Take Action to Further Improve Coordination and Information-Sharing Efforts " (GAO-09-227). We appreciate GAO's efforts in reviewing the Bank Secrecy Act (BSA) programs of all financial regulators and the report's acknowledgment of the improvements IRS has made in its BSA compliance programs since the 2006 report.

We agree the Internal Revenue Service (IRS) has important responsibilities in combating money laundering and other financial crimes and concur with your recommendations. Actions to address the recommendation to coordinate our BSA examinations with state regulators are already underway. We are also working with states to standardize the information reporting required by the various state memoranda of understanding.

The report also includes two additional recommendations that impact the IRS. The first is a joint recommendation for FinCEN and federal regulators to engage in nonpublic discussions of BSA examination procedures. We support this recommendation and look forward to participating in these discussions. The other recommends the Director, FinCEN "work with the Commissioner of IRS to establish a mutually agreed-upon policy that provides a timeframe for making enforcement decisions based on IRS referrals." We agree with this recommendation and will work closely with FinCEN to develop acceptable timeframes.

If you have any questions, or if you would like to discuss this response in more detail, please contact me or Beth Elfrey, Director, Fraud/BSA at (202) 622-4699.

Sincerely,

Linda E. Stiff

Linda E. Stiff

Enclosure

Enclosure

GAO Recommendations and IRS Corrective Actions to
GAO Draft Report: BANK SECRECY ACT:
Federal Agencies Should Take Action to Further Improve
Coordination and Information-Sharing Efforts
GAO-09-227

Recommendation: To reduce the potential for duplicative efforts and better leverage limited examination resources, we recommend that the Commissioner of IRS work with state agencies to develop a process by which to coordinate MSB examination schedules between IRS and state agencies that conduct BSA examinations of MSBs.

Comments: Small Business/Self-Employed (SB/SE), Bank Secrecy Act (BSA) agrees to develop a process for conducting joint BSA examinations with the states and to standardize the reporting format for states under their memoranda of understanding (MOUs) to optimize resources when conducting BSA examinations of money services businesses (MSBs).

Recommendation: Further, to build on improvements made in examination processes vital to ensuring BSA compliance, we recommend that the heads of FinCEN, the Federal Reserve, FDIC, OTS, OCC, NCUA, SEC, CFTC, and IRS consider developing or using an existing process to conduct regular, nonpublic discussion of BSA examination procedures and findings across all financial regulators. We recommend that the heads of SEC and CFTC consider including SROs that conduct BSA examinations.

Comments: SB/SE BSA agrees to participate in exploring the development or use of existing processes to conduct regular, nonpublic discussion of BSA examination procedures and findings. As administrator of the BSA regulatory structure, we will look to Financial Crimes Enforcement Network (FinCEN) to coordinate these efforts.

Recommendation: The Director, FinCEN expeditiously take the following [action]:

- work with the Commissioner of IRS to establish a mutually agreed-upon policy that provides a time frame for making enforcement decisions based upon IRS referrals;

Comments: We agree that a mutually agreed-upon policy for timely enforcement decisions on IRS referrals would be beneficial.

Appendix VI: Comments from the Board of Governors of the Federal Reserve

BOARD OF GOVERNORS
OF THE
FEDERAL RESERVE SYSTEM
WASHINGTON, D. C. 20551

ELIZABETH A. DUKE
MEMBER OF THE BOARD

February 2, 2009

Mr. Jack E. Edwards
Acting Director, Financial Markets and Community Investment
U.S. Government Accountability Office
441 G Street, NW
Washington, DC 20548

Dear Mr. Edwards:

Thank you for your letter dated January 2, 2009, with a copy of the draft GAO report entitled *Bank Secrecy Act: Federal Agencies Should Take Action to Further Improve Coordination and Information-Sharing Efforts* (GAO-09-227).

We believe the findings in the draft report are clearly set forth and generally support the recommendation that relates to the Federal Reserve, that is, that the heads of various federal agencies consider the use of an interagency process for regular, nonpublic discussion of Bank Secrecy Act examination procedures and findings across all financial regulators. The Federal Reserve agrees with GAO's observation that such discussions could build on improvements already made in examination processes and that there could be a benefit in regular discussion of examination procedures and general compliance trends reflected in findings at supervised institutions.

As noted in the draft report, there are existing processes for interagency communication that could serve as a venue for interagency discussion. Federal Reserve staff currently utilizes various channels to effectively communicate with other state and federal regulators regarding BSA compliance issues and will carefully consider development of these channels to regularize these discussions.

We appreciate the opportunity to review the draft report and recommendations. Please note that Federal Reserve staff has separately provided GAO staff with minor technical corrections to certain data in the draft report relating to Federal Reserve supervisory activities.

Sincerely yours,

Elizabeth A. Duke

APPENDIX VII: COMMENTS FROM THE FEDERAL DEPOSIT INSURANCE CORPORATION

FDIC
Federal Deposit Insurance Corporation
550 17th Street NW, Washington, D.C. 20429-9990 Office of the Chairman

February 2, 2009

Jack E. Edwards, Acting Director
Financial Markets and Community Investment
U.S. Government Accountability Office
441 G Street, NW
Washington, D. C. 20548

Dear Mr. Edwards:

Thank you for the opportunity to review and comment on the Government Accountability Office's (GAO) report entitled, *Bank Secrecy Act – Federal Agencies Should Take Action to Further Improve Coordination and Information-Sharing Efforts (GAO-09-0227)*. In this report, the GAO was asked to: (1) describe how Bank Secrecy Act (BSA) compliance and enforcement responsibilities are distributed; (2) describe how agencies other than the Financial Crimes Enforcement Network (FinCEN) are implementing those responsibilities and evaluate their coordination efforts; and (3) evaluate how FinCEN is implementing its BSA responsibilities.

Only one recommendation pertains to the federal banking agencies. The GAO recommends the FDIC, Board of Governors of the Federal Reserve, FinCEN, National Credit Union Administration, Office of the Comptroller of the Currency, Office of Thrift Supervision, U.S. Securities and Exchange Commission, U.S. Commodity Futures Trading Commission, and Internal Revenue Service consider developing or using an existing process to conduct regular, nonpublic discussions of BSA examination procedures and findings across all financial regulators. The FDIC agrees that periodic meetings with all federal agencies responsible for BSA compliance, examinations, and enforcement can promote consistency and coordination in examination and enforcement approaches and help reduce regulatory burden.

Sincerely,

Sheila C. Bair

Sheila C. Bair
Chairman

Appendix VIII: Comments from the Office of the Comptroller of the Currency

Comptroller of the Currency
Administrator of National Banks

Washington, DC 20219

February 4, 2009

Mr. Jack E. Edwards
Acting Director, Financial Markets and Community Investment
United States Government Accountability Office
Washington, DC 20548

Dear Mr. Edwards:

We have received and reviewed your draft report titled "Bank Secrecy Act: Federal Agencies Should Take Action to Further Improve Coordination and Information-Sharing Efforts." Your report responds to a Congressional request for a review of implementation of the Bank Secrecy Act (BSA) by the Financial Crimes Enforcement Network (FinCEN) and other federal agencies.

You are reporting that FinCEN administers the BSA framework, under which many regulatory entities, including the Office of the Comptroller of the Currency (OCC), exercise delegated and independent compliance and enforcement authorities. You report further that FinCEN provides some outreach and regulatory support but could improve information-sharing efforts. Among your recommendations, you recommend that FinCEN, the OCC, the Federal Reserve System (Board), the Federal Deposit Insurance Corporation, Office of Thrift Supervision, the National Credit Union Administration, the Securities and Exchange Commission, the Commodity Futures Trading Commission, and the Internal Revenue Service consider developing or using an existing process to conduct regular, nonpublic discussion of BSA examinations and procedures across all financial regulators.

We agree and, as noted in your report, there are a number of processes in place and groups established for the purposes of sharing information and collaboration. We will continue to participate in these initiatives and look for opportunities to share our practices and observations, to the extent permissible, with non-banking financial regulators in these or other forums.

We appreciate the opportunity to comment on the draft report.

Sincerely,

John C. Dugan
Comptroller of the Currency

APPENDIX IX: COMMENTS FROM THE OFFICE OF THRIFT SUPERVISION

Office of Thrift Supervision
Department of the Treasury *John M. Reich, Director*
1700 G Street, N.W., Washington, DC 20552 • (202) 906-6590 • (202) 898-0230

February 2, 2009

Jack E. Edwards
Acting Director, Financial Markets and
Community Investment
United States Government Accountability Office
441 G Street, NW
Washington, DC 20548

Dear Mr. Edwards:

Thank you for the opportunity to review and comment on the Government Accountability Office (GAO)'s draft report entitled, *Federal Agencies Should Take Action to Further Improve Coordination and Information-Sharing Efforts (GAO 09-227).* The report reviews how responsibility for ensuring compliance with the Bank Secrecy Act (BSA) is distributed among various agencies; describes how various agencies are implementing their responsibilities and evaluates their coordination efforts; and evaluates how the Financial Crimes Enforcement Network (FinCEN) is implementing its BSA responsibilities. As the report notes, the federal agencies have made significant progress in their coordinated efforts to address BSA and anti-money laundering (AML) compliance at the institutions they supervise.

GAO makes several recommendations directed to FinCEN, the Internal Revenue Service (IRS), and other federal agencies. Among the recommendations is for FinCEN, IRS and the federal financial regulators to consider developing a mechanism to regularly discuss BSA examinations and procedures across all regulators. While the Office of Thrift Supervision (OTS) currently works closely with the Office of the Comptroller of the Currency, Federal Deposit Insurance Corporation, Board of Governors of the Federal Reserve System and National Credit Union Administration (collectively the federal banking agencies) and FinCEN on BSA related matters, OTS will collaborate with other regulators with BSA/AML responsibilities to consider a method to discuss BSA examinations and procedures. The federal banking agencies and FinCEN have established a number of formal committees and working groups to promote collaboration on BSA issues and we are strongly committed to ensuring that the institutions we supervise are in compliance with BSA/AML requirements.

Thank you for your efforts.

Sincerely,

John M. Reich

APPENDIX X: COMMENTS FROM NATIONAL CREDIT UNION ADMINISTRATION

National Credit Union Administration

Office of the Chairman

February 3, 2009

Jack E. Edwards
Acting Director
Financial Markets and Community Investment
U.S. Government Accountability Office
441 G St., NW
Washington, DC 20548

Dear Mr. Edwards:

Thank you for the opportunity to review and comment on the Government Accountability Office's (GAO) draft report entitled, *Bank Secrecy Act: Federal Agencies Should Take Action to Further Improve Coordination and Information-Sharing Efforts (GAO-09-227)*. This report reviews how the Bank Secrecy Act (BSA) compliance and enforcement responsibilities are distributed amongst the federal and state regulatory agencies; describes how these agencies implement those responsibilities and evaluates their coordination efforts; and evaluates how the Financial Crimes Enforcement Network (FinCEN) is implementing its BSA responsibilities.

The GAO recommends that FinCEN, the federal financial regulators, and the Internal Revenue Service (IRS) consider developing or using an existing process to conduct regular, nonpublic discussion of BSA examination procedures and findings across all financial regulators. The federal banking agencies and FinCEN regularly meet to discuss BSA regulations, examination policies and procedures, training, and compliance matters. The National Credit Union Administration (NCUA) will work with these agencies to consider developing a process to discuss BSA procedures with the IRS and the other financial regulators.

The NCUA remains strongly committed to our role in ensuring that credit unions are in compliance with the requirements of the BSA. To this end, we will continue to work with the other financial regulators to promote collaboration on BSA examination matters.

Sincerely,

Michael E. Fryzel
Chairman
National Credit Union Administration

EI/JAG:jag

1775 Duke Street - Alexandria, VA 22314-3428 - 703-518-6300

Appendix XI: Comments from Securities and Exchange Commission

UNITED STATES
SECURITIES AND EXCHANGE COMMISSION
WASHINGTON, D.C. 20549

OFFICE OF COMPLIANCE
INSPECTIONS AND
EXAMINATIONS

February 2, 2009

Jack E. Edwards
Acting Director
Financial Markets and Community Investment
U.S. Government Accountability Office
441 G Street, N.W.
Washington, D.C. 20548

Dear Mr. Edwards:

Thank you for the opportunity to review and comment on the General Accountability Office's ("GAO") draft report entitled: Bank Secrecy Act: Federal Agencies Should Take Action to Further Improve Coordination and Information-Sharing Efforts ("Report"). The Report describes how Bank Secrecy Act ("BSA") compliance oversight responsibility is distributed among federal and state regulators, self regulatory organizations ("SROs") and the Financial Crimes Enforcement Network ("FinCEN"). The Report further describes how these entities are implementing their respective BSA responsibilities and coordinating efforts among one another. The SEC is proud to be one of the federal agencies tasked with implementing the BSA's anti-money laundering requirements for broker-dealers and mutual funds, and with the SROs, we have taken steps to establish an aggressive and coordinated AML examination program.

The GAO makes two recommendations that relate to the SEC: 1) that FinCEN expeditiously finalize and implement a data-access agreement with SROs that conduct BSA/AML examinations, and 2) that FinCEN and the other federal agencies, including the SEC, consider developing a mechanism for sharing information regarding BSA/AML (anti-money laundering) examination procedures and findings. We agree with both of these recommendations.

As noted in the Report, the Financial Industry Regulatory Authority ("FINRA"), the SRO that conducts the majority of securities broker-dealer examinations, does not have direct electronic access to BSA data and must instead request the data from the SEC or FinCEN. Direct access to BSA data would permit FINRA to more effectively use its AML resources to take a more risk-based approach to identifying firms, and areas within a firm's AML program, that required examination. We hope that FinCEN will provide SROs such as FINRA with direct electronic access to BSA data in a form that will be broad enough to allow them to properly risk-scope their examinations and effectively leverage resources, as specifically discussed and recommended in the Report.

In addition, you recommend that FinCEN and the other federal agencies, including the SEC, consider developing a mechanism for sharing information regarding

Jack E. Edwards
February 2, 2009
Page 2

BSA/AML (anti-money laundering) examination procedures and findings. We recognize that effective cooperation can evolve over time and appreciate your suggestions for improvement. We agree that regulators would benefit from the development of a mechanism through which all financial regulators can discuss, on a regular non-public basis, BSA/AML examination procedures and findings. To this end, FinCEN plans to hold, and the SEC plans to attend, a meeting in February 2009 to discuss with other federal regulators possible methods for achieving this goal.

Thank you again for the opportunity to comment on the Report. We also would like to express our appreciation for the courtesy you and your staff extended to us during this review.

Sincerely,

Lori A. Richards
Director
Office of Compliance Inspections and Examinations

APPENDIX XII: COMMENTS FROM THE COMMODITY FUTURES TRADING COMMISSION

U.S. Commodity Futures Trading Commission
Three Lafayette Centre, 1155 21st Street, NW, Washington, DC 20581
www.cftc.gov

Michael V. Dunn
Acting Chairman

February 3, 2009

Jack Edwards
Acting Director
Financial Markets and Community Investment
Government Accountability Office
441 G St., NW
Washington, DC 20548

Dear Mr. Edwards:

We have received and reviewed the Government Accountability Office's draft report titled "Bank Secrecy Act: Federal Agencies Should Take Action to Further Improve Coordination and Information-Sharing Efforts." We commend your staff for their hard work on this detailed report and thank you for providing the Commodity Futures Trading Commission ("CFTC") with the opportunity to provide comments. CFTC staff is separately providing technical comments to GAO staff; the below comments will focus on the report's recommendations.

Several of the report's recommendations are of particular relevance to the CFTC. First, the report recommends that the Financial Crimes Enforcement Network ("FinCEN"), which administers the Bank Secrecy Act ("BSA"), and the federal agencies to which it has delegated examination authority consider developing a mechanism to share information on BSA examination procedures and findings to better ensure consistency in the application of the BSA, identify any cross-industry concerns, and leverage each other's expertise. Second, the report recommends that FinCEN expeditiously finalize and implement an information-sharing Memorandum of Understanding ("MOU") with the CFTC. Finally, the report recommends that FinCEN finalize and implement a data-access MOU with the CFTC and the self-regulatory organizations (SROs) conducting BSA/AML examinations.

As to the first recommendation, the CFTC supports all efforts to increase cooperation among regulators in this area. We would be pleased to participate in any discussions that bring us together with other federal financial regulators and allow us to share our experiences and expertise in developing and implementing BSA examination procedures.

As to the second and third recommendations, the draft report notes throughout that FinCEN and CFTC have been involved in extensive negotiations regarding information-sharing and data access MOUs. The report also indicates that the two agencies expect to conclude negotiations in mid-January. We are pleased to report that on January 15, 2009, FinCEN and CFTC finalized and signed two memoranda of understanding concerning, respectively, information sharing and BSA database access.

The first MOU provides for mutual information sharing between FinCEN and the CFTC ("Information-Sharing MOU") and sets forth procedures for the exchange of information between FinCEN and the CFTC. As a general matter, under this MOU the CFTC will provide FinCEN with information relating to the policies and procedures of the CFTC and the SROs that directly examine CFTC-regulated entities for BSA compliance, and FinCEN will provide information to the CFTC about FinCEN's administration of the BSA.

The second MOU ("Data Access MOU") sets forth the terms under which the CFTC can gain access to information collected pursuant to the reporting authority of the BSA ("BSA Database"). Generally, the Data Access MOU allows authorized CFTC personnel to make direct electronic inquiries to retrieve information from the BSA Database and to use that information as appropriate in the exercise of the CFTC's regulatory authority, including BSA examination authority that is implemented through oversight of the futures SROs. We believe that these two agreements will enhance the CFTC's ability to effectively implement its BSA examination responsibilities, conduct oversight of the futures markets, and meet its enforcement mission.

Thank you again for providing us with the opportunity to comment on this important report.

Sincerely yours,

Michael V. Dunn

Michael V. Dunn
Acting Chairman

ABBREVIATIONS

AML	anti-money laundering
BSA	Bank Secrecy Act of 1970
BSAAG	Bank Secrecy Act Advisory Group
CFTC	Commodity Futures Trading Commission
CIP	customer identification program
CMP	civil money penalty
CMS	Case Management System
CTR	currency transaction report
FDIC	Federal Deposit Insurance Corporation
Federal Reserve	Board of Governors of the Federal Reserve System
FFIEC	Federal Financial Institutions Examination Council
FINRA	Financial Industry Regulatory Authority
FinCEN	Financial Crimes Enforcement Network
IRS	Internal Revenue Service
Justice	Department of Justice
MOU	memorandum of understanding
MSB	money services business
NBFI	nonbank financial institution
NCUA	National Credit Union Administration
NFA	National Futures Association
OCC	Office of the Comptroller of the Currency
OCIE	Office of Compliance Inspections and Examinations
OTS	Office of Thrift Supervision
RPPD	Regulatory Policy and Programs Division
SAR	suspicious activity report
SEC	Securities and Exchange Commission
SRO	self-regulatory organization
Treasury	Department of the Treasury

End Notes

[1] Pub. L. No. 91-508, 84 Stat. 1114 (1970) (codified as amended in 12 U.S.C. §§ 1829(b), 1951-1959; 31 U.S.C. §§ 5311-5330).

[2] The Uniting and Strengthening America by Providing Appropriate Tools Required to Intercept and Obstruct Terrorism Act of 2001, Pub. L. No. 107-56, 115 Stat. 272 (2001). We refer to this act as the "USA PATRIOT Act." MSBs are defined by regulation to include any person

conducting business of more than $1,000 with the same person on the same day in any one of the following activities: currency dealing or exchange; check cashing; issuing, selling, or redemption of traveler's checks, money orders, or stored value cards; or provision of money transfer services in any amount. 31 C.F.R. § 103. 11(uu). For the purposes of this document, "futures firms" refer to futures commission merchants and introducing brokers.

[3] Throughout the report we will use the term "federal banking regulators" to refer collectively to the Federal Reserve, FDIC, OCC, OTS, and NCUA.

[4] SROs are nongovernmental entities responsible for regulating their members through the adoption and enforcement of rules and regulations governing the business conduct of their members. Both exchanges and membership organizations, such as the National Futures Association (NFA) and the Financial Industry Regulatory Authority (FINRA), are SROs. For the futures industry, the SROs must designate one SRO as the lead regulator for compliance audits (examinations) when a futures commission merchant is a member of more than one SRO. For the purposes of this report, SROs also will refer to designated SROs.

[5] GAO, *Bank Secrecy Act: Opportunities Exist for FinCEN and the Banking Regulators to Further Strengthen the Framework for Consistent BSA Oversight*, GAO-06-386 (Washington, D.C.: Apr. 28, 2006); *USA PATRIOT ACT: Additional Guidance Could Improve Implementation of Regulations Related to Customer Identification and Information Sharing Procedures*, GAO-05-412 (Washington, D.C.: May 6, 2005).

[6] GAO, *Financial Regulation: Industry Challenges Prompt Need to Reconsider U.S. Regulatory Structure*, GAO-05-61 (Washington, D.C.: Oct. 6, 2004).

[7] GAO, *Results-Oriented Government: Practices That Can Help Enhance and Sustain Collaboration Among Federal Agencies*, GAO-06-15 (Washington, D.C.: Oct. 21, 2005).

[8] Pub. L. No. 99-570, title I, subtitle H, 100 Stat. 3207-17 (1986).

[9] Pub. L. No. 99-570, 100 Stat. 3207 (1986).

[10] Pub. L. No. 102-550, title XV, §1517(b), 106 Stat. 3672 (1992).

[11] The USA PATRIOT Act requires all financial institutions to have AML programs unless they are exempted by FinCEN as provided in the act. Pub. L. No. 107-56 § 352. In 2002 and 2003, FinCEN published rule proposals that would have required commodity trading advisors, investment advisers, and "unregistered investment companies" to have AML programs, but these proposals were withdrawn recently pending further consideration by FinCEN. See 73 Fed. Reg. 65567 (Nov. 4, 2008, commodity trading advisors); 73 Fed. Reg. 65568 (Nov. 4, 2008, investment advisers); 73 Fed. Reg. 65570 (Nov. 4, 2008, "unregistered investment companies," defined to include certain hedge funds, commodity pools, and real estate investment trusts that are not subject to federal functional regulation).

[12] Pub. L. No. 107-56 § 365(a).

[13] 31 C.F.R. § 103.56. The regulation delegates examination authority to SEC for securities broker-dealers and investment companies. The delegation to CFTC pertains to futures commission merchants, introducing brokers, and commodity trading advisors.

[14] *See, e.g.*, 12 U.S.C. §§ 1818(s) (requiring federal banking agencies to promulgate BSA regulations and conduct BSA examinations), 1786(q) (applying the same requirement to NCUA). See Procedures for Monitoring Bank Secrecy Act (BSA) Compliance, 12 C.F.R. § 208.63 (Federal Reserve), 12 C.F.R. § 326, subpart B, (FDIC), 12 C.F.R. § 748.2, (NCUA), 12. C.F.R., (OCC), 12 C.F.R. § 563.177 (OTS). SEC and CFTC have authority to examine the entities they regulate for compliance with the respective agency's regulations, and those regulations require compliance with BSA and its implementing regulations.

[15] The regulations authorize the Assistant Secretary of Enforcement in Treasury to impose civil penalties for BSA violations. 31 C.F.R. § 103.57.

[16] *See* 12 U.S.C. §§ 1818(b), (s) (institutions other than credit unions), 1786(b), (q) (federally insured credit unions).

[17] 31 C.F.R. § 103.56(g).

[18] 12 U.S.C. § 1818(s).

[19] 12 U.S.C. § 1786(q).

[20] State-chartered commercial banks that are members of the Federal Reserve are subject to supervision by that regulator. Other state-chartered banks, such as nonmember state banks, and state savings banks, with federally insured deposits are subject to FDIC oversight, while OTS supervises state-chartered savings associations insured by FDIC and federally chartered savings associations. Federally chartered institutions are subject to oversight by their chartering agencies. Generally, OCC supervises national banks and NCUA supervises federally chartered credit unions.

[21] Beginning in 2004, state banking departments, federal banking regulators, and FinCEN increased coordination on BSA-related examination and information-sharing activities; and the federal banking regulators began training state examiners to review for BSA compliance. See GAO-06-386.

[22] 17 C.F.R. §240.17a-8, issued by SEC, requires registered brokers-dealers to comply with the reporting, record-keeping, and record retention requirements of the regulations adopted under BSA (which include SAR requirements and customer identification programs), and 17 C.F.R. § 270.38a-1 requires mutual funds to establish and implement compliance programs that include provisions for compliance with AML regulations. Similarly, CFTC regulation 17 C.F.R. § 42.2 issued by CFTC, requires futures commission merchants and introducing brokers to comply with the applicable provisions of BSA and FinCEN regulations.

[23] FINRA is the result of the 2007 consolidation of the former National Association of Securities Dealers and the member regulation, enforcement, and arbitration operations of New York Stock Exchange Regulation, Inc.

[24] In addition to conducting the majority of broker-dealer examinations, FINRA officials said they have several regulatory agreements in place where they conduct regulatory work (which would include BSA/AML examinations) on behalf of other SROs. They told us the other securities SROs that conduct their own BSA/AML compliance examinations review entities for BSA/AML compliance that are generally options market makers that do not have retail customers.

[25] The only types of examination, other than BSA/AML, that IRS conducts are tax audits.

[26] 31 C.F.R. § 103.56(b)(8).

[27] In April 2003, FinCEN signed a memorandum of agreement with IRS, in which it delegated its enforcement authority for the Foreign Bank Account Reports to IRS. The reporting requirements, which are grounded in the BSA, authorize FinCEN to require residents or citizens of the United States (or a person in, and doing business in, the United States) to keep records and file reports concerning transactions with any foreign financial institutions. IRS may assess and collect civil penalties for noncompliance with the Foreign Bank Account Reports requirements, investigate possible civil violations, employ summons power, issue administrative rulings, and take any other action reasonably necessary for enforcement of these provisions, including pursuit of injunctions.

[28] SEC staff said SEC and SROs began examining broker-dealers informally for BSA/AML procedures in 2001, prior to the implementation of the USA PATRIOT Act. SEC developed the first BSA/AML module for broker-dealers in 2002. Other securities SROs—which conduct about 10 percent of broker-dealer examinations—do not use the SEC-FINRA module but have their own procedures. FINRA officials told us that other SROs examine institutions that generally do not have retail customers.

[29] We reviewed SEC and SRO examination modules for broker-dealers and SEC's modules for mutual funds, but as they are nonpublic we cannot discuss their contents.

[30] The Joint Audit Committee is a committee of U.S. futures exchanges and regulatory organizations. One of its responsibilities is to determine the practices and procedures to be followed by each SRO in the conduct of audits of futures commission merchants. NFA's BSA/AML module differs slightly in that it does not include procedures for clearing members as it does not examine these types of institutions. A clearing member of an

exchange has the ability to process and settle trades. Nonclearing members must process and settle all trades through a clearing member.

[31] The group provides a framework for the sharing of information and the coordination of regulatory efforts among exchanges that trade securities and related products. SEC, CFTC, and securities and futures SROs participate in this group.

[32] *GAO, Bank Secrecy Act: FinCEN and IRS Need to Improve and Better Coordinate Compliance and Data Management Efforts*, GAO-07-212 (Washington, D.C.: Dec. 15, 2006).

[33] The coordinated NBFI strategy outlines the following objectives: (1) evaluating the MSB regulatory framework, (2) better identifying the NBFI population, (3) better selecting the NBFI population, (4) supporting risk-based examinations, and (5) outreach.

[34] The Money Transmitter Regulators Association consists of state regulatory authorities for money transmitters and sellers of traveler's checks, money orders, drafts, and other money instruments.

[35] GAO-06-15.

[36] The BSAAG, in addition to its annual plenary meetings, has various subcommittee meetings, including meetings on banking, insurance, law enforcement, SARs, and securities and futures.

[37] GAO-06-15.

[38] The authority of the federal banking regulators to take an enforcement action includes, among other things, an action based upon an institution's violation of any law. *See, e.g.,* 12 U.S.C. §S 1818, 1786.

[39] Informal and formal actions vary by banking regulator. For example, among the available remedies, OCC may issue a notice of deficiency for failure to comply with applicable safety and soundness internal control standards in the BSA area, while FDIC may enter into an MOU to address a similar deficiency.

[40] The banking regulators use different terms to classify problems associated with elements of institutions' BSA/AML programs. For example, some of the banking regulators use "deficiency" and others "violation." Also, the 2007 FFIEC interagency statement does not clearly distinguish between a deficiency and a violation, although it provides examples of when either deficiencies or violations can lead to the issuance of a cease-and-desist order.

[41] OCC does not share jurisdiction with state regulators, but OCC officials said they do share pertinent information with some state agencies. State agencies have the authority to taken enforcement actions against institutions chartered within their state that are in violation of banking legislation.

[42] CFTC uses "enforcement action," while its SROs use "disciplinary action." For the purposes of this report, we will use "enforcement action" for both.

[43] NFA, which has been delegated registration duties by CFTC, additionally may condition or revoke the registration of any futures firm.

[44] In 2003, Treasury delegated enforcement authority for compliance with foreign bank and financial accounts reporting to IRS.

[45] The Internal Revenue Manual provides guidance on the IRS referral procedures and determination processes.

[46] Often, criminal investigations of individuals are traced to a specific financial institution. During the initial investigation, if it becomes apparent that certain financial institutions are being used to launder money, investigators will look at the level of criminal proceeds laundered through the institution and the circumstances surrounding the activity and then determine if a separate investigation should be opened on the institution. Investigators subsequently assess whether the institution had sufficient systems in place to detect and prevent criminal activity.

[47] FinCEN has been studying the feasibility and effect of implementing a BSA-based crossborder wire transfer reporting requirement.

[48] 31 U.S.C. § 5318. The same provision authorizes Treasury generally to delegate BSA duties and powers to appropriate agencies that supervise financial institutions subject to BSA requirements.

[49] 68 F.R. 25149 (May 9, 2003). The BSA requirement is set forth at 31 U.S.C. § 5318(l). Subsection (h) of that same provision calls for FinCEN to consult with the regulators, should FinCEN promulgate regulations setting minimum standards for AML programs. FinCEN's AML regulations for financial institutions, which apply to futures commission merchants and introducing brokers, are set forth at 31 C.F.R. § 103.120.

[50] According to CFTC officials, some futures commission merchants asserted that the applicability of the rule, 31 C.F.R. § 103.123, was not clear with respect to which futures commission merchant—the executing or clearing broker—in a give-up arrangement had the CIP responsibilities. A give-up transaction occurs when a broker executes an order on an exchange for a customer and then submits the trade for clearing with another futures commission merchant (clearing broker).

[51] Financial Crimes Enforcement Network Commodity Futures Trading Commission Guidance FIN-2007-G001 (Apr. 20, 2007).

[52] This work addressed a prior GAO recommendation that FinCEN and the federal banking regulators work together to ensure that emerging BSA/AML risks are communicated effectively to examiners and the industry through updates of the manual and other guidance. See GAO-06-386.

[53] FinCEN considers the results of these surveys to be nonpublic information. FinCEN reports on the "understandability" of its guidance as a performance measure in its annual report, and therefore these public results are included in this report. In the 2006 survey, 94 percent of respondents rated the guidance from FinCEN's Regulatory Resource Center as understandable. In the 2007 and 2008 surveys, 91 percent and 94 percent, respectively, rated guidance as understandable. In all 3 years, the vast majority of respondents were financial institutions and the remaining respondents were regulators or other interested parties. Despite some potential limitations associated with the surveys, after review we concluded that the overall frequencies for survey questions should be sufficiently valid and reflected the overall opinions of those surveyed.

[54] As of October 2008, FinCEN said it had held six on-site visits with large institutions in support of this initiative.

[55] CMS is a vendor-provided software product delivered through a secure Web portal.

[56] FinCEN officials said that the Office of Compliance generates three reports from CMS on a monthly basis—a consolidated monthly status report, a count of cases by date recorded, and a count of cases by closed date. The Office of Enforcement downloads a CMS report on a quarterly basis to calculate the average time to process enforcement cases, which is a public performance measure.

[57] Cases are grouped in CMS by the federal regulator with delegated examination authority for the referred institution.

[58] As stated previously, FinCEN delegated its enforcement authority for the Foreign Bank Account Reports to IRS. A Letter 1112 is issued if violations are found during an examination. The letter details the violations and asks that the entity commit to correcting the apparent violations.

[59] IRS officials will then provide the facts of the case, a summary of the examination, and violation information in their referral to FinCEN. IRS examiners do not recommend the type of enforcement action, penalty, or dollar amount to FinCEN.

[60] For example, in August 2007, FinCEN, the Federal Reserve, and Justice issued coordinated civil and criminal BSA-related enforcement actions against American Express on the same day.

[61] In May 2004, FinCEN and OCC concurrently imposed $25 million in CMPs against Riggs Bank, N.A. for willful and systemic BSA violations. See GAO-06-386.

[62] For example, in late 2005, FDIC imposed a cease-and-desist order against Israel Discount Bank in conjunction with the New York State Department of Banking, and in 2006 followed up by issuing a CMP in conjunction with the New York State Department of Banking and FinCEN. In April 2006, OTS, FinCEN, and Justice took coordinated civil and criminal BSA enforcement actions against BankAtlantic.

[63] GAO-06-386.

[64] Form 8300s are similar to CTRs. For IRS-supervised entities, they must report cash payments of more than $10,000 using Form 8300s.

[65] The Office of Management and Budget conducted this assessment in 2006 using its Program Assessment Rating Tool—a standard series of questions meant to serve as a diagnostic performance tool. The agency draws on available program performance and evaluation information to form conclusions about program benefits and recommend adjustments that may improve results.

[66] FinCEN considers most of the results of this survey to be nonpublic information. The survey-derived information included in this report is a publicly available performance measure that FinCEN developed based on questions from its 2008 survey of the holders of information-sharing MOUs. Despite some potential limitations associated with the survey, after review we concluded that the overall frequencies for survey questions should be sufficiently valid and reflected the overall opinions of those surveyed.

[67] In response to a recommendation we made in GAO-07-212, FinCEN officials said they, in collaboration with IRS, have been developing a long-term comprehensive plan for re-engineering BSA data management activities. FinCEN expects implementation of the plan to take from 3 to 5 years.

[68] A 3 14(a) hit refers to a bank identifying one of its customers as matching an entity included on the biweekly list that FinCEN distributes in accordance with section 314(a) of the USA PATRIOT Act to financial institutions of individuals, entities, and organizations engaged in or reasonably suspected of engaging in terrorist acts or money laundering activities.

[69] These other reports include the Designation of an Exempt Person, Report of Foreign Bank and Financial Account Forms, and Report of International Currency of Monetary Instrument Forms.

[70] GAO, *Results-Oriented Government: Practices That Can Help Enhance and Sustain Collaboration Among Federal Agencie*s, GAO-06-15 (Washington, D.C.: Oct. 21, 2005).

[71] State-chartered commercial banks that are members of the Federal Reserve are subject to supervision by that regulator. Other state-chartered banks, such as nonmember state banks, and state savings banks, with federally insured deposits are subject to FDIC oversight, while OTS supervises state-chartered savings associations insured by FDIC and federally chartered savings associations. Federally chartered institutions are subject to oversight by their chartering agencies. Generally, OCC supervises national banks and NCUA supervises federally chartered credit unions.

[72] SEC uses the term "deficiency" to refer to potential violations of specific statutory or regulatory requirements, and "weakness" to refer to concerns that do not rise to the level of a deficiency.

[73] GAO, *Bank Secrecy Act: FinCEN and IRS Need to Improve and Better Coordinate Compliance and Data Management Efforts*, GAO-07-212 (Washington, D.C.: Dec. 15, 2006).

INDEX

D

E

F

G

H

I

J

L

P

Q

R

S